TEEN

CROSSWORD
PUZZLE

FUN THEMED QUICK CROSSWORDS
FOR TEEN BOYS AND GIRLS

WITH
BONUS
PRITABLE
COLORING
PAGES

B N WILLIAM

PUBLISH

BONUS

DEAR CUSTOMER,
THANK YOU FOR PURCHASING OUR BOOK. AS A TOKEN OF GRATITUDE, WE'RE OFFERING YOU **30 CHRISTMAS COLORING PAGES** TO PRINT AT HOME AND ENJOY.
HAVE FUN COLORING WITH YOUR FAMILY THIS HOLIDAY SEASON! IF YOU LOVED OUR PRODUCT, **PLEASE CONSIDER LEAVING A REVIEW ON AMAZON. YOUR SUPPORT HELPS OUR SMALL BUSINESS GROW.** THANKS FOR CHOOSING US AND HAPPY COLORING!

DOWLOAD HERE

A SPECIAL REQUEST !

JOIN US FOR MORE! SCAN THE QR CODE TO CONNECT WITH US ONLINE AND SIGN UP FOR OUR NEWSLETTER. GET READY FOR EXCLUSIVE BONUSES AND EXCITING UPDATES. SCAN, SUBSCRIBE, AND ENJOY! THANK YOU ! ❤

SCAN ME

DIY Fashion

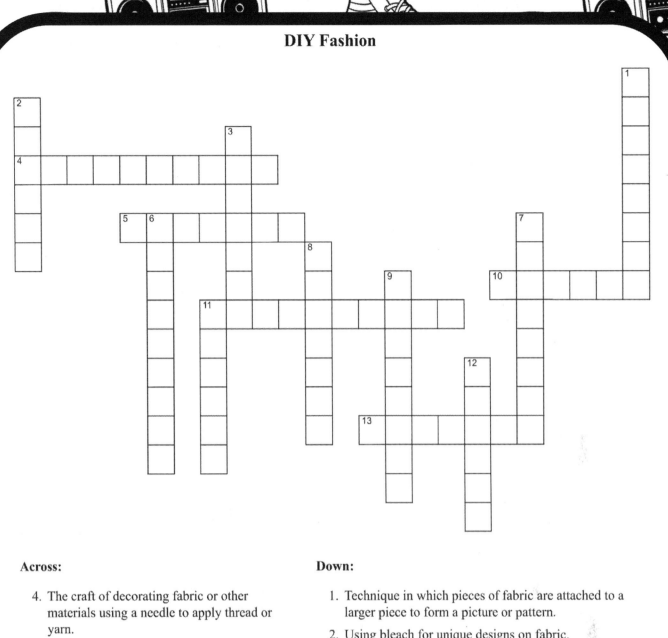

Across:

4. The craft of decorating fabric or other materials using a needle to apply thread or yarn.

5. Taking old clothes and transforming them into something new.

10. A popular trend in DIY fashion involving vibrant colors.

11. Applying a design or pattern to clothes using a thin sheet of cardboard or metal.

13. Adding beads to clothing for decoration.

Down:

1. Technique in which pieces of fabric are attached to a larger piece to form a picture or pattern.

2. Using bleach for unique designs on fabric.

3. A process of creating textiles by using a crochet hook to interlock loops of yarn, thread, or strands of other materials.

6. Sewing together pieces of fabric into a larger design.

7. Making garments or fabric by interlocking loops of wool or other yarn with knitting needles.

8. A form of textile produced using knotting techniques.

9. Making clothes look aged and worn as a fashion statement.

11. Adding small, shiny disks to fabric for a sparkly effect.

12. Adding a decorative border of threads to clothing.

Current Events

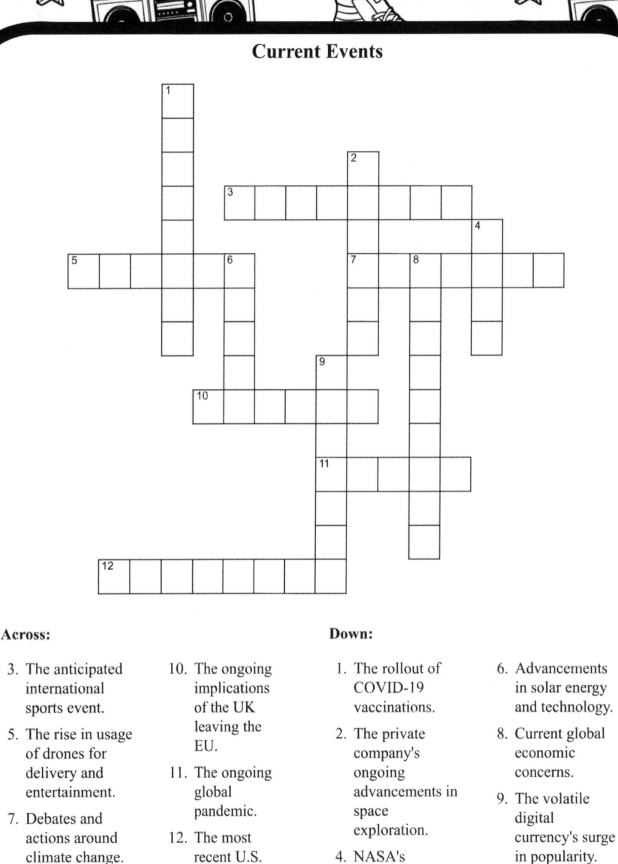

Across:

3. The anticipated international sports event.

5. The rise in usage of drones for delivery and entertainment.

7. Debates and actions around climate change.

10. The ongoing implications of the UK leaving the EU.

11. The ongoing global pandemic.

12. The most recent U.S. Presidential election.

Down:

1. The rollout of COVID-19 vaccinations.

2. The private company's ongoing advancements in space exploration.

4. NASA's Perseverance rover's successful landing.

6. Advancements in solar energy and technology.

8. Current global economic concerns.

9. The volatile digital currency's surge in popularity.

Mental Health Awareness

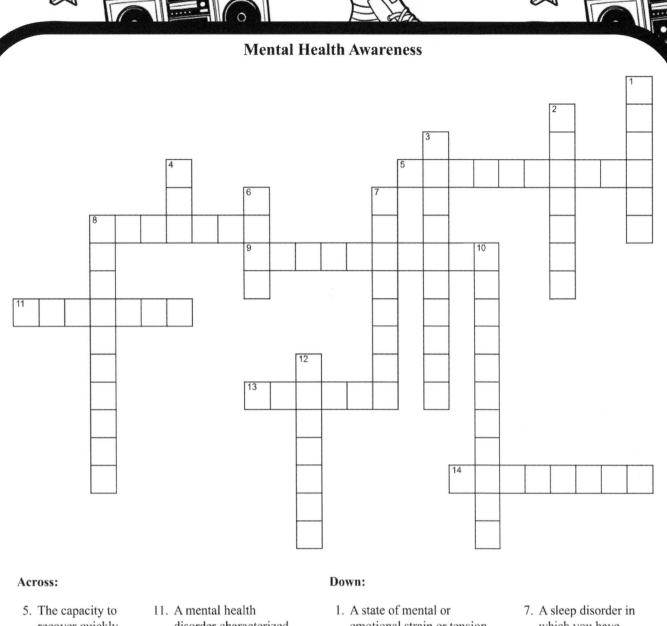

Across:

5. The capacity to recover quickly from difficulties; mental toughness.

8. A set of attitudes or beliefs held by someone.

9. Confidence in one's own worth or abilities; self-respect.

11. A mental health disorder characterized by feelings of worry or fear.

13. A mark of disgrace associated with a particular circumstance, quality, or person, often related to mental health.

14. The practice of taking action to preserve or improve one's own health.

Down:

1. A state of mental or emotional strain or tension resulting from adverse or demanding circumstances.

2. Treatment intended to relieve or heal a disorder.

3. A mood disorder that causes a persistent feeling of sadness and loss of interest.

4. Short for obsessive-compulsive disorder, a chronic disorder in which a person has uncontrollable, reoccurring thoughts and behaviors.

6. Short for post-traumatic stress disorder, a disorder that develops after a terrifying ordeal involving physical harm or the threat of physical harm.

7. A sleep disorder in which you have trouble falling and/or staying asleep.

8. A practice where an individual uses a technique to achieve a mentally clear and emotionally calm state.

10. The practice of focusing one's attention on the present moment.

12. A disorder associated with episodes of mood swings ranging from depressive lows to manic highs.

Book Genres

Across:

4. A genre that provides a description or account of someone's life.

9. A genre that features a protagonist on a quest or exploring new territories.

10. A genre that uses aesthetic and rhythmic qualities of language to evoke meanings.

11. A genre intended to scare, unsettle or horrify the reader.

12. Short for science fiction, this genre deals with imaginative and futuristic concepts.

13. A genre that places its primary focus on the relationship and romantic love between two people.

14. A collection of memories that an individual writes about moments or events that took place in their life.

Down:

1. A genre of fiction that commonly uses magic and other supernatural phenomena as a primary plot element.

2. A genre that uses suspense, tension, and excitement as its main elements.

3. A genre of fiction that deals with the solution of a crime or the unraveling of secrets.

5. A genre set in the late 18th to late 19th century in the American western frontier.

6. A genre that uses humor, irony, exaggeration, or ridicule to expose and criticize people's stupidity or vices.

7. A genre that uses in-depth development of realistic characters dealing with emotional themes.

8. A genre that explores social and political structures in a dark, nightmare world.

Cooking Tips

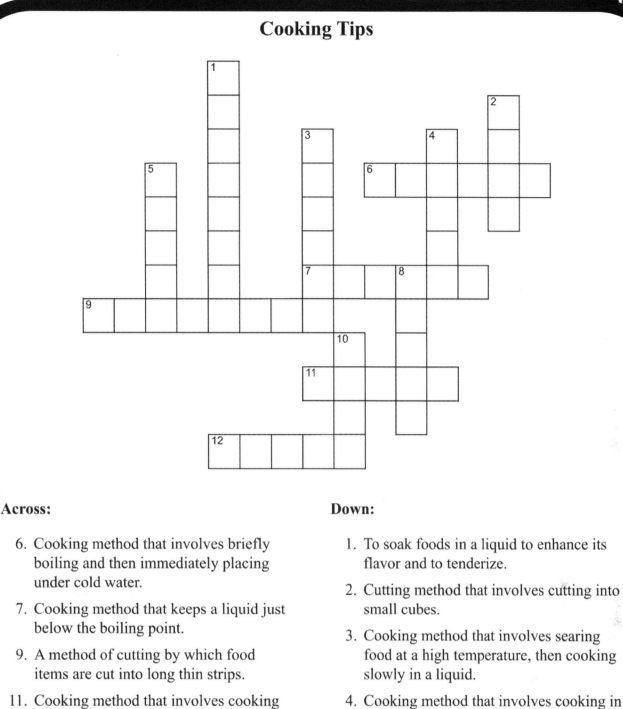

Across:

6. Cooking method that involves briefly boiling and then immediately placing under cold water.

7. Cooking method that keeps a liquid just below the boiling point.

9. A method of cutting by which food items are cut into long thin strips.

11. Cooking method that involves cooking by submerging food in a liquid, such as water or broth.

12. A method used in baking to work dough into a uniform mixture.

Down:

1. To soak foods in a liquid to enhance its flavor and to tenderize.

2. Cutting method that involves cutting into small cubes.

3. Cooking method that involves searing food at a high temperature, then cooking slowly in a liquid.

4. Cooking method that involves cooking in a small amount of fat.

5. Cooking method that involves applying heat directly from above the food.

8. Cutting method that involves cutting into very small pieces.

10. A method of gently incorporating ingredients.

Young Musicians

Across:

1. BTS, the South Korean boy band that has gained worldwide popularity.

2. Joji, the Japanese singer-songwriter known for his lo-fi music.

4. Rosalía, the Spanish singer known for her contemporary flamenco music.

6. Khalid, the American singer-songwriter known for his soulful sound.

8. Olivia Rodrigo, a singer and songwriter who became popular with her debut single "drivers license".

9. Cardi B, the American rapper known for her hits "Bodak Yellow" and "WAP".

10. Lil Nas X, the American rapper known for his country-rap hit "Old Town Road".

11. Megan Thee Stallion, the American rapper known for her hits "Savage" and "WAP".

Down:

1. Billie Eilish, the Grammy-winning singer known for her unique sound.

3. Tate McRae, the Canadian singer-songwriter known for her hit "you broke me first".

5. Shawn Mendes, the Canadian singer-songwriter known for his hits like "Stitches" and "Treat You Better".

7. Doja Cat, the American singer and rapper known for her viral hit "Say So".

9. Conan Gray, the American singer-songwriter known for his hit "Heather".

Youth Cultures

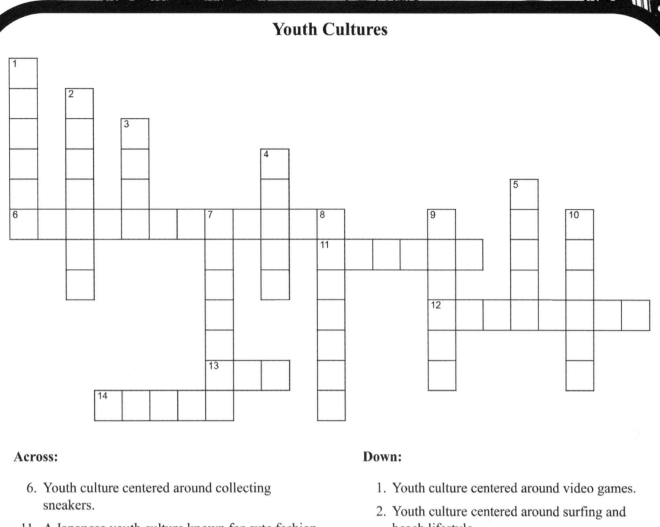

Across:

6. Youth culture centered around collecting sneakers.

11. A Japanese youth culture known for cute fashion and pop culture.

12. Youth culture known for vintage styles, indie music, and a preference for non-mainstream lifestyle.

13. Youth culture known for emotional music and introspective fashion.

14. Youth culture known for dark, often black clothing, pale complexion with colored hairstyles, and gothic rock music.

Down:

1. Youth culture centered around video games.

2. Youth culture centered around surfing and beach lifestyle.

3. Youth culture known for aggressive hard rock, hair dyed in bright colors, and a rebellious attitude.

4. Youth culture centered around intense interest in anime and manga.

5. Youth culture known for academic, technological, and cultural interests.

7. Youth culture known for peace activism, psychedelic music, and bohemian fashion.

8. Youth culture centered around skateboarding.

9. Youth culture that appreciates hip hop music and urban culture.

10. Youth culture known for listening to electronic dance music and attending rave parties.

College Sports Teams

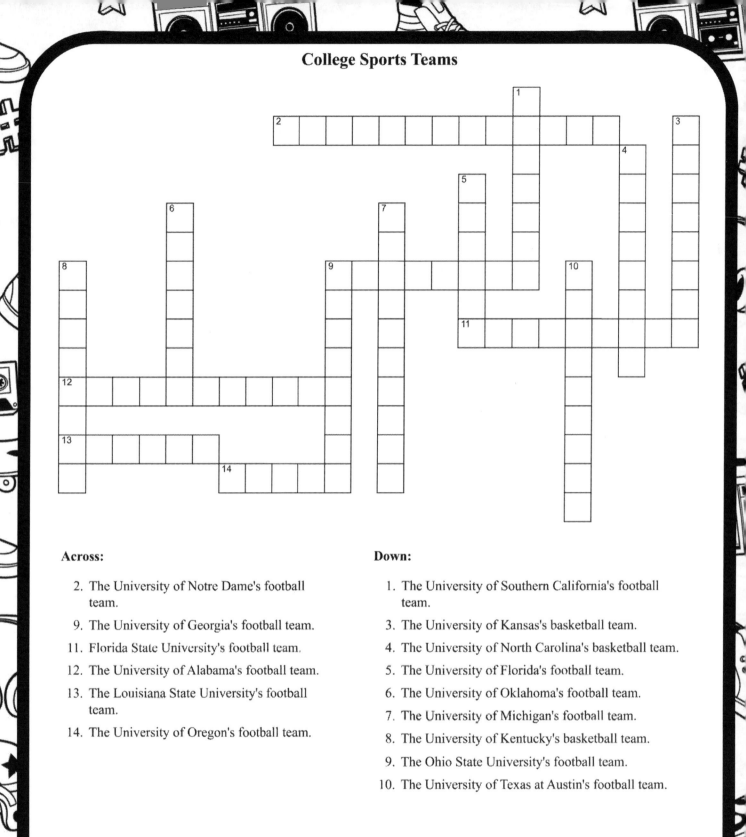

Across:

2. The University of Notre Dame's football team.
9. The University of Georgia's football team.
11. Florida State University's football team.
12. The University of Alabama's football team.
13. The Louisiana State University's football team.
14. The University of Oregon's football team.

Down:

1. The University of Southern California's football team.
3. The University of Kansas's basketball team.
4. The University of North Carolina's basketball team.
5. The University of Florida's football team.
6. The University of Oklahoma's football team.
7. The University of Michigan's football team.
8. The University of Kentucky's basketball team.
9. The Ohio State University's football team.
10. The University of Texas at Austin's football team.

Popular Hashtags

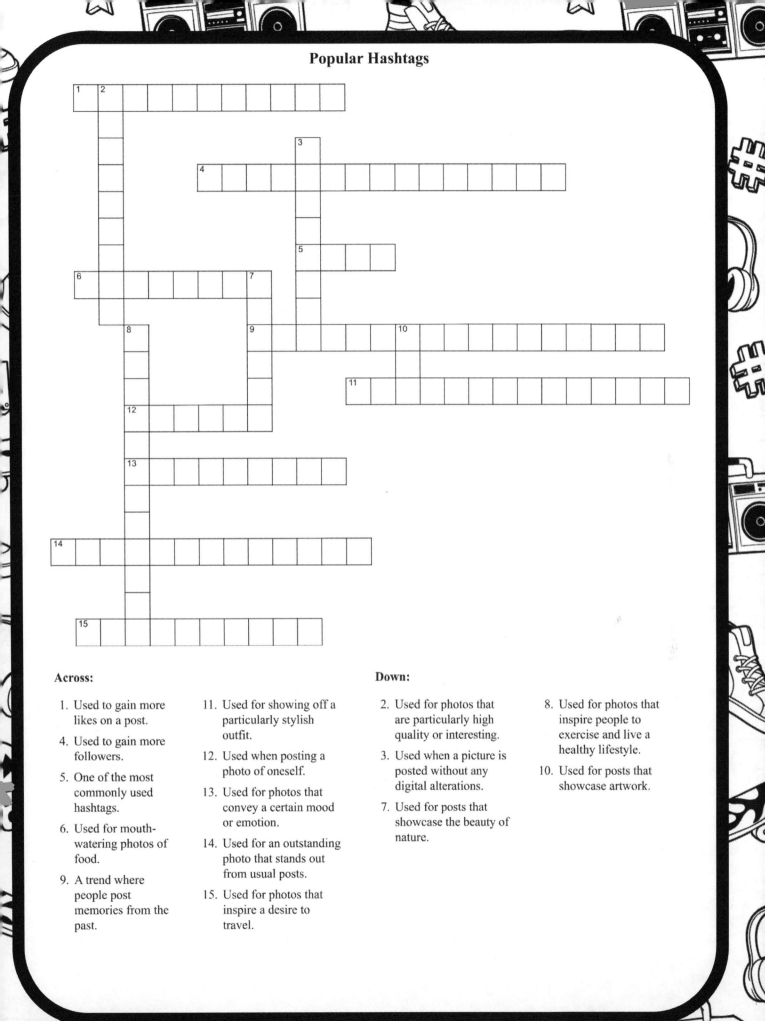

Across:

1. Used to gain more likes on a post.

4. Used to gain more followers.

5. One of the most commonly used hashtags.

6. Used for mouth-watering photos of food.

9. A trend where people post memories from the past.

11. Used for showing off a particularly stylish outfit.

12. Used when posting a photo of oneself.

13. Used for photos that convey a certain mood or emotion.

14. Used for an outstanding photo that stands out from usual posts.

15. Used for photos that inspire a desire to travel.

Down:

2. Used for photos that are particularly high quality or interesting.

3. Used when a picture is posted without any digital alterations.

7. Used for posts that showcase the beauty of nature.

8. Used for photos that inspire people to exercise and live a healthy lifestyle.

10. Used for posts that showcase artwork.

Space Exploration

Across:

2. A private aerospace manufacturer and space transportation company.

3. A NASA space probe orbiting Jupiter.

5. The government body responsible for space activities in Russia.

7. The United States' space agency.

10. The first artificial Earth satellite, launched by the Soviet Union.

11. A celestial body that orbits the sun and has a "tail" of gas and dust.

12. The fourth planet from the sun, known for its red appearance.

14. A NASA mission to study the planet Jupiter and its moons.

Down:

1. The second planet from the sun, known for its extreme temperatures.

4. A spacecraft built by NASA for human deep space exploration.

6. A NASA mission to Saturn, providing a wealth of data about the planet, its rings, and its moons.

8. A space telescope that has been providing images of space since 1990.

9. A NASA mission to discover Earth-size planets orbiting other stars.

13. The NASA program that resulted in human exploration of the moon.

Dating Apps

Across:

3. An U.S.-based, internationally operating online dating app.

7. An online dating website designed specifically to match single men and women for long-term relationships.

9. A dating app designed to be deleted.

10. A private, membership-based social network application for dating.

11. A dating app for gay, bi, trans, and queer people.

Down:

1. One of the oldest online dating services.

2. A dating app that learns as you click to pair you with singles.

4. A dating service known as "Plenty of Fish".

5. A dating app where women make the first move.

6. A location-based social search mobile app that allows users to like or dislike other users.

8. A dating app for LGBTQ+ women.

9. A dating app that shows you people you've crossed paths with.

Drawing Techniques

Across:

2. A method that focuses on the light and dark areas of a drawing.

3. Using an eraser to bring out highlights and correct mistakes.

5. A simple and spontaneous way of drawing.

6. Technique of using small dots to simulate varying degrees of solidity or shading.

9. A method of drawing by capturing the form, movement, and pose.

10. Creating tonal or shading effects with closely spaced parallel lines.

11. A technique that involves applying a very light coat of pencil for texture.

12. The technique of drawing the perceived edges of a form.

13. Using intersecting parallel lines for shading.

14. A simple, loosely drawn type of drawing.

Down:

1. Smoothly transitioning from one color or tone to another.

4. The process of adding color, shading, and lamination to a 2-D or 3-D wireframe.

7. Copying a drawing, or part of it, by following the lines on a superimposed transparent sheet.

8. A technique of depicting volumes and spatial relationships on a flat surface.

Mindfulness Practices

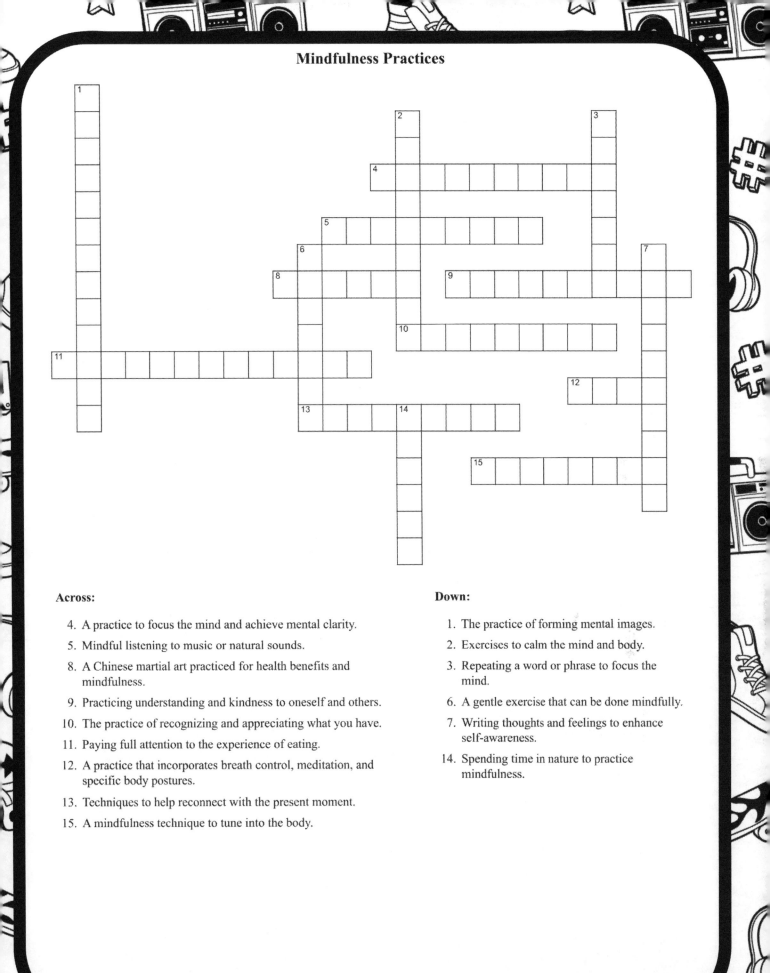

Across:

4. A practice to focus the mind and achieve mental clarity.

5. Mindful listening to music or natural sounds.

8. A Chinese martial art practiced for health benefits and mindfulness.

9. Practicing understanding and kindness to oneself and others.

10. The practice of recognizing and appreciating what you have.

11. Paying full attention to the experience of eating.

12. A practice that incorporates breath control, meditation, and specific body postures.

13. Techniques to help reconnect with the present moment.

15. A mindfulness technique to tune into the body.

Down:

1. The practice of forming mental images.

2. Exercises to calm the mind and body.

3. Repeating a word or phrase to focus the mind.

6. A gentle exercise that can be done mindfully.

7. Writing thoughts and feelings to enhance self-awareness.

14. Spending time in nature to practice mindfulness.

Language Learning

Across:

2. An app that connects language learners with native speakers.

3. A language learning program that focuses on listening and speaking skills.

6. An app that uses visuals to teach languages.

10. An app that connects you with native speakers to practice languages.

11. An app that turns web pages into language learning lessons

Down:

1. An app for learning languages through conversation.

4. An app that offers daily lessons in 33 languages.

5. A software for learning languages, "Rosetta Stone".

7. A platform that teaches languages through videos.

8. A community-based app for learning languages.

9. A flashcard app used for language learning.

Gaming Consoles

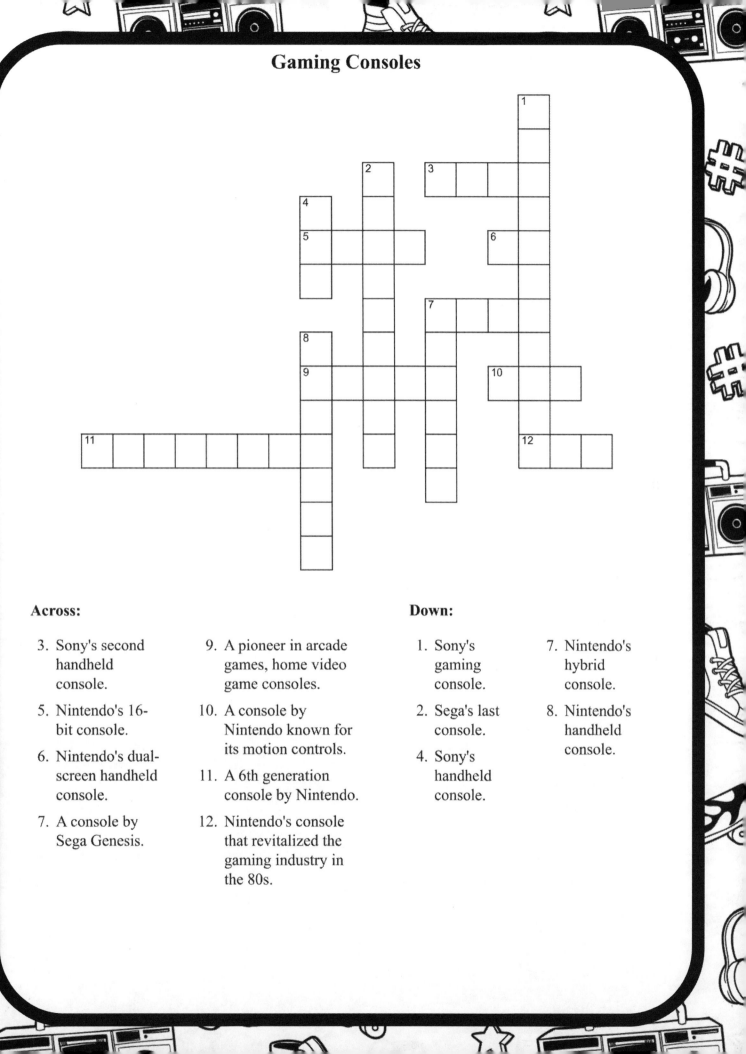

Across:

3. Sony's second handheld console.

5. Nintendo's 16-bit console.

6. Nintendo's dual-screen handheld console.

7. A console by Sega Genesis.

9. A pioneer in arcade games, home video game consoles.

10. A console by Nintendo known for its motion controls.

11. A 6th generation console by Nintendo.

12. Nintendo's console that revitalized the gaming industry in the 80s.

Down:

1. Sony's gaming console.

2. Sega's last console.

4. Sony's handheld console.

7. Nintendo's hybrid console.

8. Nintendo's handheld console.

Thriller Movies

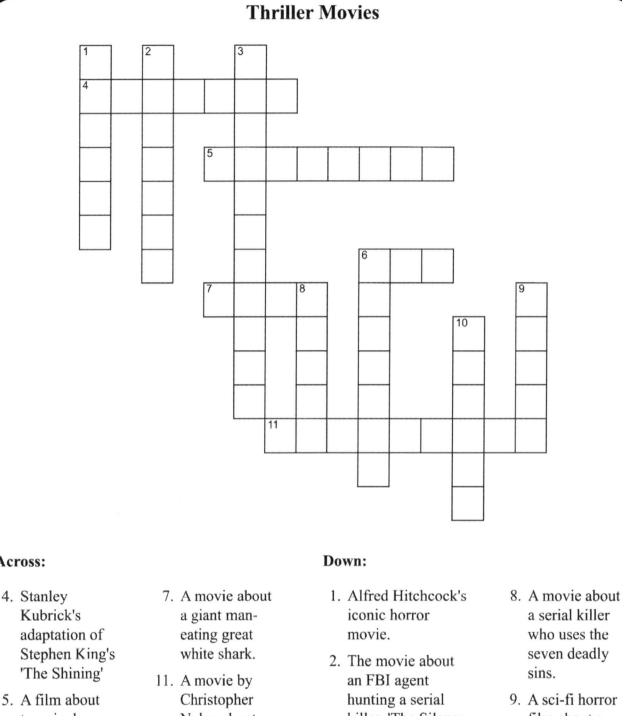

Across:

4. Stanley Kubrick's adaptation of Stephen King's 'The Shining'

5. A film about two rival magicians by Christopher Nolan.

6. A gory film about a serial killer who designs deadly traps.

7. A movie about a giant man-eating great white shark.

11. A movie by Christopher Nolan about dreams within dreams.

Down:

1. Alfred Hitchcock's iconic horror movie.

2. The movie about an FBI agent hunting a serial killer, 'The Silence of the Lambs'

3. A movie about a man who learns he has superpowers.

6. A horror movie set in Thailand.

8. A movie about a serial killer who uses the seven deadly sins.

9. A sci-fi horror film about a deadly creature in a spaceship.

10. A movie about the hunt for the Zodiac killer.

Young Adult Classics

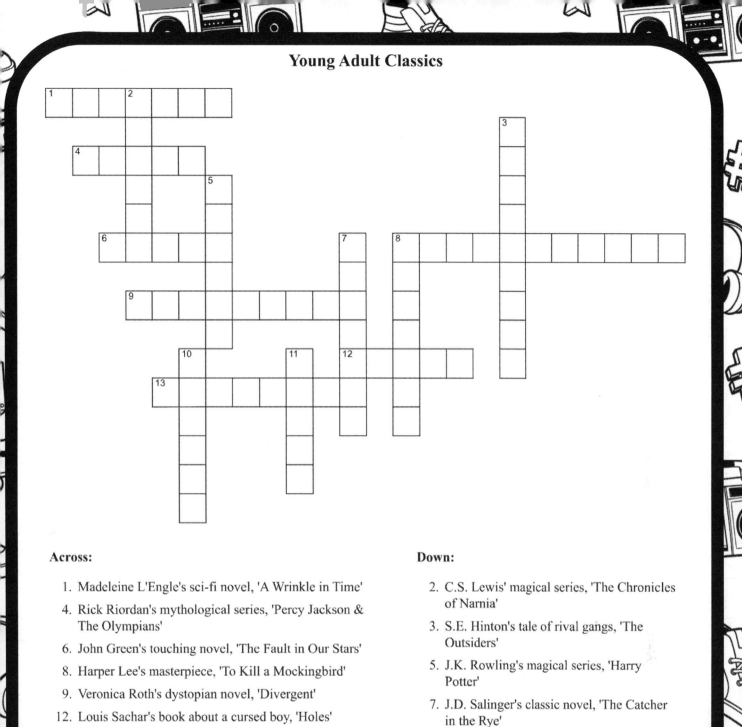

Across:

1. Madeleine L'Engle's sci-fi novel, 'A Wrinkle in Time'
4. Rick Riordan's mythological series, 'Percy Jackson & The Olympians'
6. John Green's touching novel, 'The Fault in Our Stars'
8. Harper Lee's masterpiece, 'To Kill a Mockingbird'
9. Veronica Roth's dystopian novel, 'Divergent'
12. Louis Sachar's book about a cursed boy, 'Holes'
13. Neil Gaiman's creepy novella, 'Coraline'

Down:

2. C.S. Lewis' magical series, 'The Chronicles of Narnia'
3. S.E. Hinton's tale of rival gangs, 'The Outsiders'
5. J.K. Rowling's magical series, 'Harry Potter'
7. J.D. Salinger's classic novel, 'The Catcher in the Rye'
8. Roald Dahl's book about a precocious girl, 'Matilda'
10. J.R.R. Tolkien's epic adventure, 'The Hobbit'
11. Lois Lowry's dystopian novel, 'The Giver'

Fitness Apps

Across:

1. An app for tracking running workouts.

5. An app for fitness and nutrition.

7. An app for workout classes.

8. An app to accompany Fitbit's line of fitness trackers.

10. An app for tracking food intake and exercise.

12. An app offering yoga classes.

13. An app for meditation and sleep.

Down:

2. A social fitness network app.

3. A health app for planning meals and tracking calories.

4. A fitness app created by Australian personal trainer Kayla Itsines.

6. A workout tracking app.

8. A fitness app that creates a daily and deeply personalized workout routine.

9. An app for meditation and mindfulness.

11. An app for tracking running and cycling.

Dream Jobs

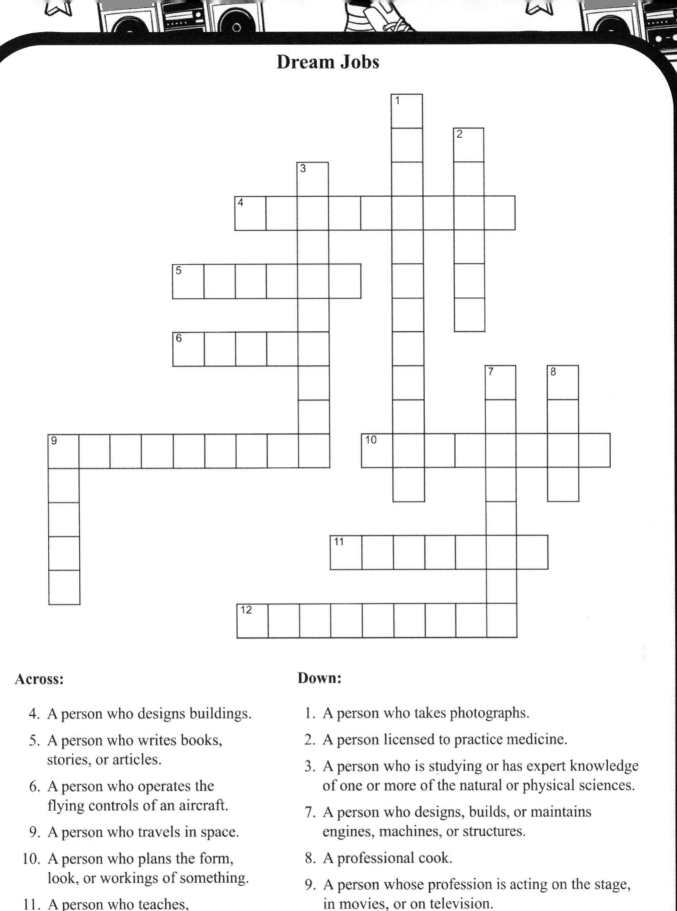

Across:

4. A person who designs buildings.

5. A person who writes books, stories, or articles.

6. A person who operates the flying controls of an aircraft.

9. A person who travels in space.

10. A person who plans the form, look, or workings of something.

11. A person who teaches, especially in a school.

12. A person (such as a director or producer) who makes movies.

Down:

1. A person who takes photographs.

2. A person licensed to practice medicine.

3. A person who is studying or has expert knowledge of one or more of the natural or physical sciences.

7. A person who designs, builds, or maintains engines, machines, or structures.

8. A professional cook.

9. A person whose profession is acting on the stage, in movies, or on television.

Travel Goals

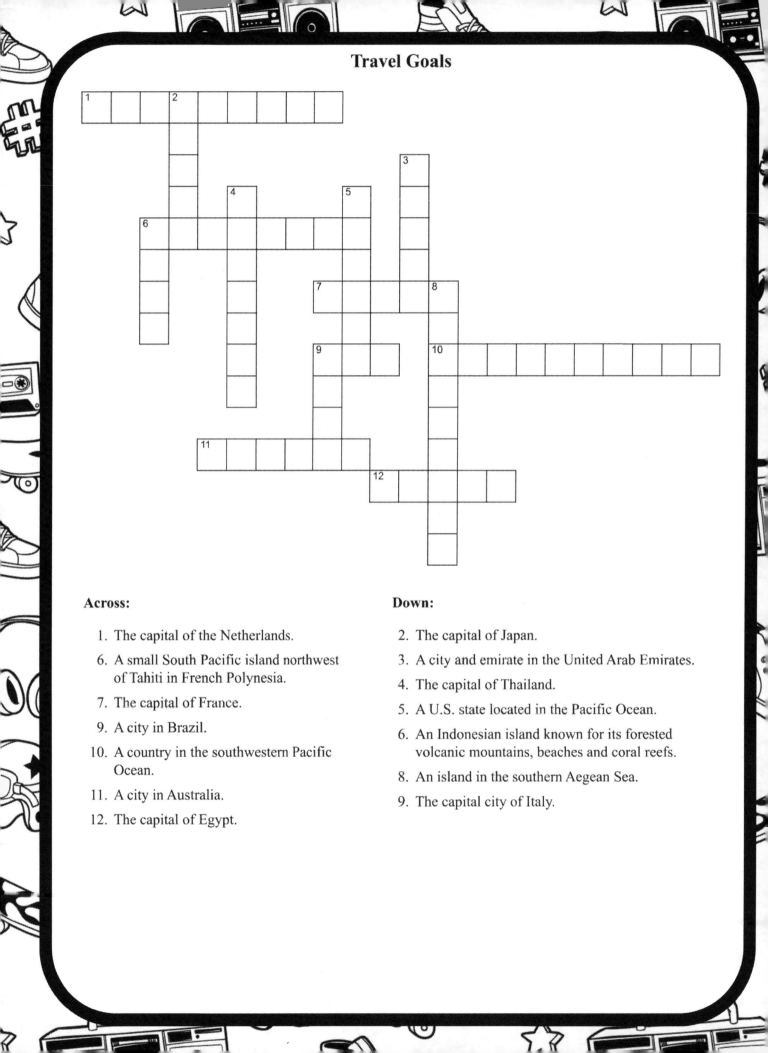

Across:

1. The capital of the Netherlands.
6. A small South Pacific island northwest of Tahiti in French Polynesia.
7. The capital of France.
9. A city in Brazil.
10. A country in the southwestern Pacific Ocean.
11. A city in Australia.
12. The capital of Egypt.

Down:

2. The capital of Japan.
3. A city and emirate in the United Arab Emirates.
4. The capital of Thailand.
5. A U.S. state located in the Pacific Ocean.
6. An Indonesian island known for its forested volcanic mountains, beaches and coral reefs.
8. An island in the southern Aegean Sea.
9. The capital city of Italy.

Study Apps

Across:

4. A platform that combines workplace chat, video meetings, and file storage.

7. A study guide website and app.

8. A free web service for schools.

9. A note-taking app.

12. An English language writing-enhancement platform.

13. A language learning app.

14. A mobile and web-based study app.

15. A non-profit educational organization.

Down:

1. An app that provides components such as notes, databases, kanban boards, wikis, calendars and reminders.

2. An online learning platform.

3. An app for learning mathematics.

5. An online course provider.

6. A spaced repetition flashcard program.

10. An online service for computing answers and providing knowledge.

11. A game-based learning platform.

Dessert Recipes

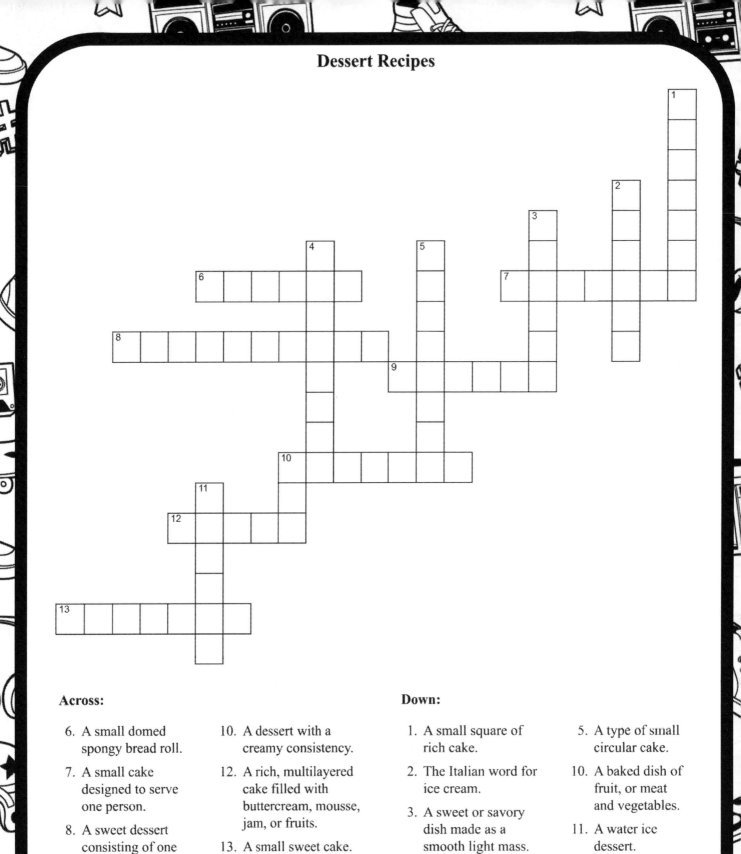

Across:

6. A small domed spongy bread roll.

7. A small cake designed to serve one person.

8. A sweet dessert consisting of one or more layers.

9. A cold dessert of sponge cake and fruit covered with layers of custard.

10. A dessert with a creamy consistency.

12. A rich, multilayered cake filled with buttercream, mousse, jam, or fruits.

13. A small sweet cake.

Down:

1. A small square of rich cake.

2. The Italian word for ice cream.

3. A sweet or savory dish made as a smooth light mass.

4. An Italian dessert made with coffee, biscuits, and mascarpone cheese.

5. A type of small circular cake.

10. A baked dish of fruit, or meat and vegetables.

11. A water ice dessert.

Cool Gadgets

Across:

4. A hybrid console that can be used as a home console and portable device.

6. A device that you wear over your eyes like a pair of goggles.

8. An unmanned aircraft or ship.

9. A mobile device with a touchscreen display.

10. A mobile phone with advanced features.

12. A series of digital media players.

14. A smart home product.

Down:

1. A wearable device that tracks your physical activity.

2. A home video game console.

3. Wireless Bluetooth earbuds.

5. High-performance audio products.

7. A self-balancing scooter.

11. A smart home security product.

13. An electronic device for reading books.

Financial Literacy

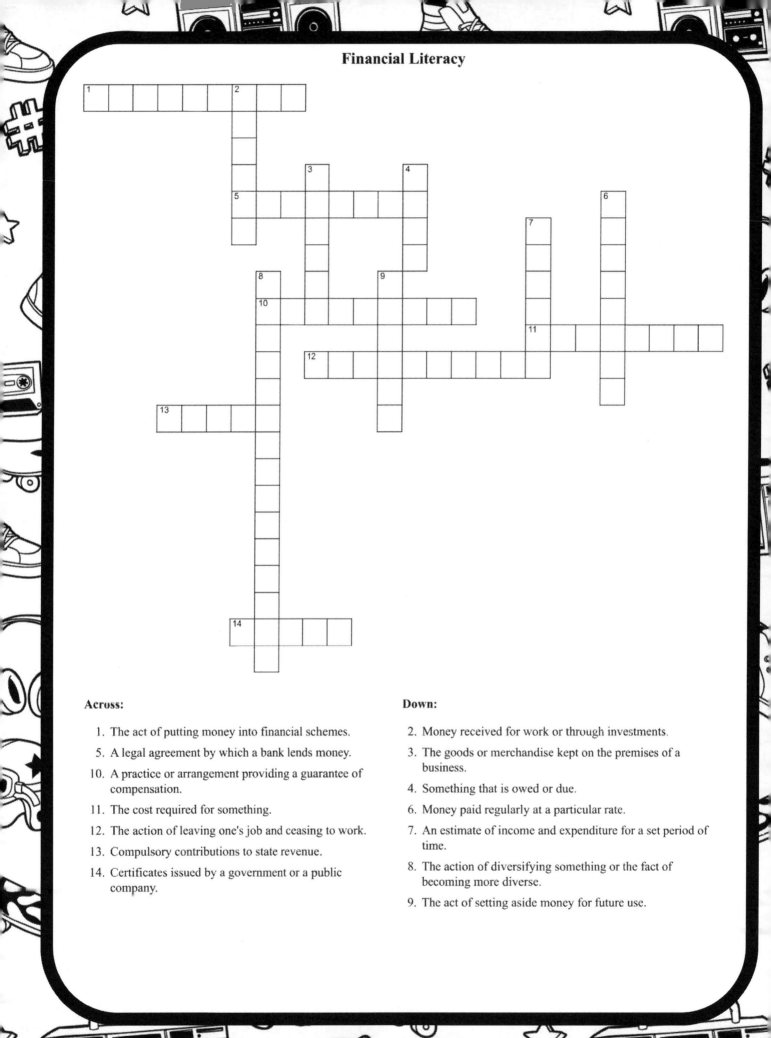

Across:

1. The act of putting money into financial schemes.

5. A legal agreement by which a bank lends money.

10. A practice or arrangement providing a guarantee of compensation.

11. The cost required for something.

12. The action of leaving one's job and ceasing to work.

13. Compulsory contributions to state revenue.

14. Certificates issued by a government or a public company.

Down:

2. Money received for work or through investments.

3. The goods or merchandise kept on the premises of a business.

4. Something that is owed or due.

6. Money paid regularly at a particular rate.

7. An estimate of income and expenditure for a set period of time.

8. The action of diversifying something or the fact of becoming more diverse.

9. The act of setting aside money for future use.

Body Positivity

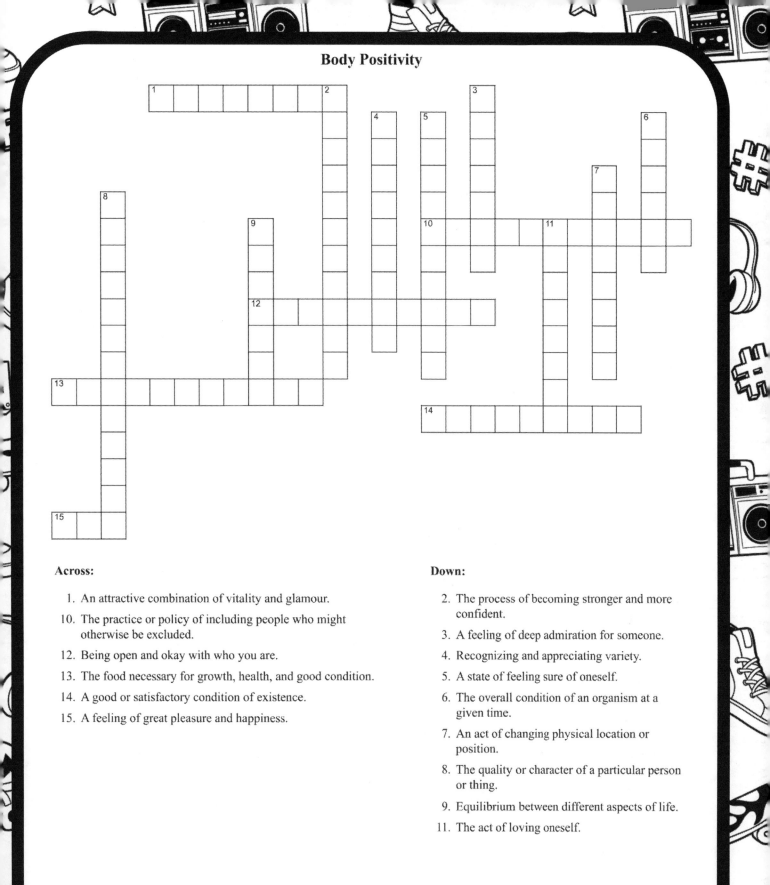

Across:

1. An attractive combination of vitality and glamour.
10. The practice or policy of including people who might otherwise be excluded.
12. Being open and okay with who you are.
13. The food necessary for growth, health, and good condition.
14. A good or satisfactory condition of existence.
15. A feeling of great pleasure and happiness.

Down:

2. The process of becoming stronger and more confident.
3. A feeling of deep admiration for someone.
4. Recognizing and appreciating variety.
5. A state of feeling sure of oneself.
6. The overall condition of an organism at a given time.
7. An act of changing physical location or position.
8. The quality or character of a particular person or thing.
9. Equilibrium between different aspects of life.
11. The act of loving oneself.

Career Options

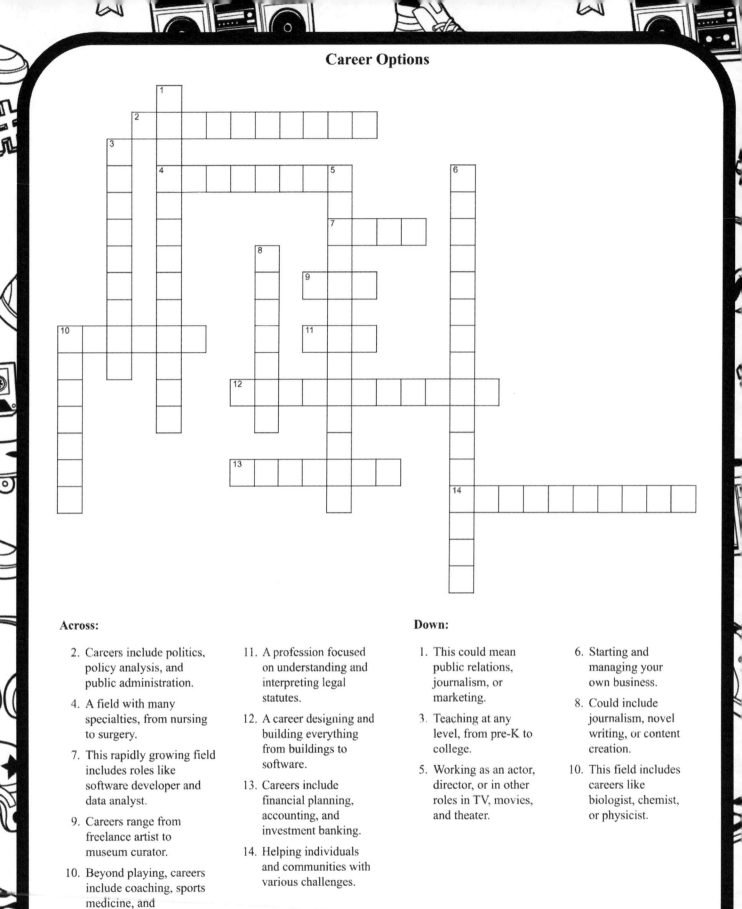

Across:

2. Careers include politics, policy analysis, and public administration.

4. A field with many specialties, from nursing to surgery.

7. This rapidly growing field includes roles like software developer and data analyst.

9. Careers range from freelance artist to museum curator.

10. Beyond playing, careers include coaching, sports medicine, and management.

11. A profession focused on understanding and interpreting legal statutes.

12. A career designing and building everything from buildings to software.

13. Careers include financial planning, accounting, and investment banking.

14. Helping individuals and communities with various challenges.

Down:

1. This could mean public relations, journalism, or marketing.

3. Teaching at any level, from pre-K to college.

5. Working as an actor, director, or in other roles in TV, movies, and theater.

6. Starting and managing your own business.

8. Could include journalism, novel writing, or content creation.

10. This field includes careers like biologist, chemist, or physicist.

College Preparation

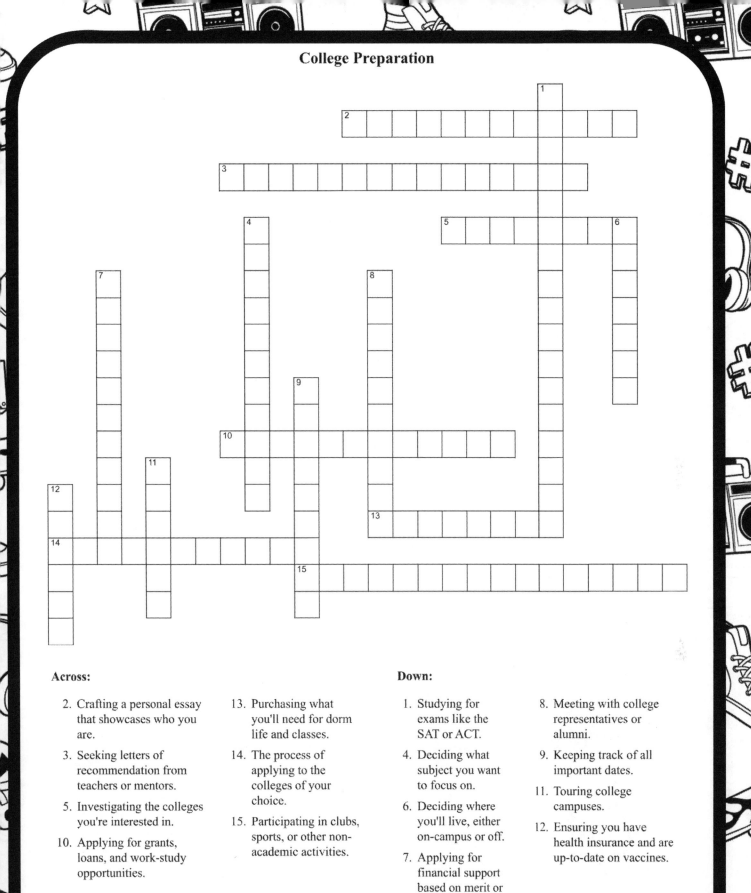

Across:

2. Crafting a personal essay that showcases who you are.

3. Seeking letters of recommendation from teachers or mentors.

5. Investigating the colleges you're interested in.

10. Applying for grants, loans, and work-study opportunities.

13. Purchasing what you'll need for dorm life and classes.

14. The process of applying to the colleges of your choice.

15. Participating in clubs, sports, or other non-academic activities.

Down:

1. Studying for exams like the SAT or ACT.

4. Deciding what subject you want to focus on.

6. Deciding where you'll live, either on-campus or off.

7. Applying for financial support based on merit or need.

8. Meeting with college representatives or alumni.

9. Keeping track of all important dates.

11. Touring college campuses.

12. Ensuring you have health insurance and are up-to-date on vaccines.

DIY Projects

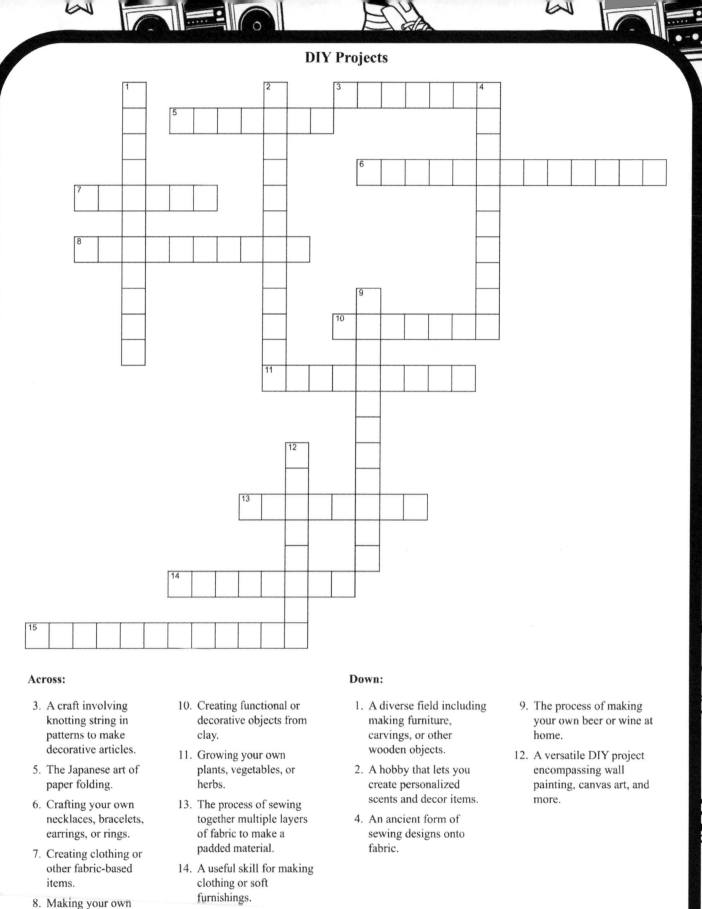

Across:

3. A craft involving knotting string in patterns to make decorative articles.

5. The Japanese art of paper folding.

6. Crafting your own necklaces, bracelets, earrings, or rings.

7. Creating clothing or other fabric-based items.

8. Making your own little ecosystem in a glass container.

10. Creating functional or decorative objects from clay.

11. Growing your own plants, vegetables, or herbs.

13. The process of sewing together multiple layers of fabric to make a padded material.

14. A useful skill for making clothing or soft furnishings.

15. Preserving and presenting photos and memories in creative ways.

Down:

1. A diverse field including making furniture, carvings, or other wooden objects.

2. A hobby that lets you create personalized scents and decor items.

4. An ancient form of sewing designs onto fabric.

9. The process of making your own beer or wine at home.

12. A versatile DIY project encompassing wall painting, canvas art, and more.

High School Musicals

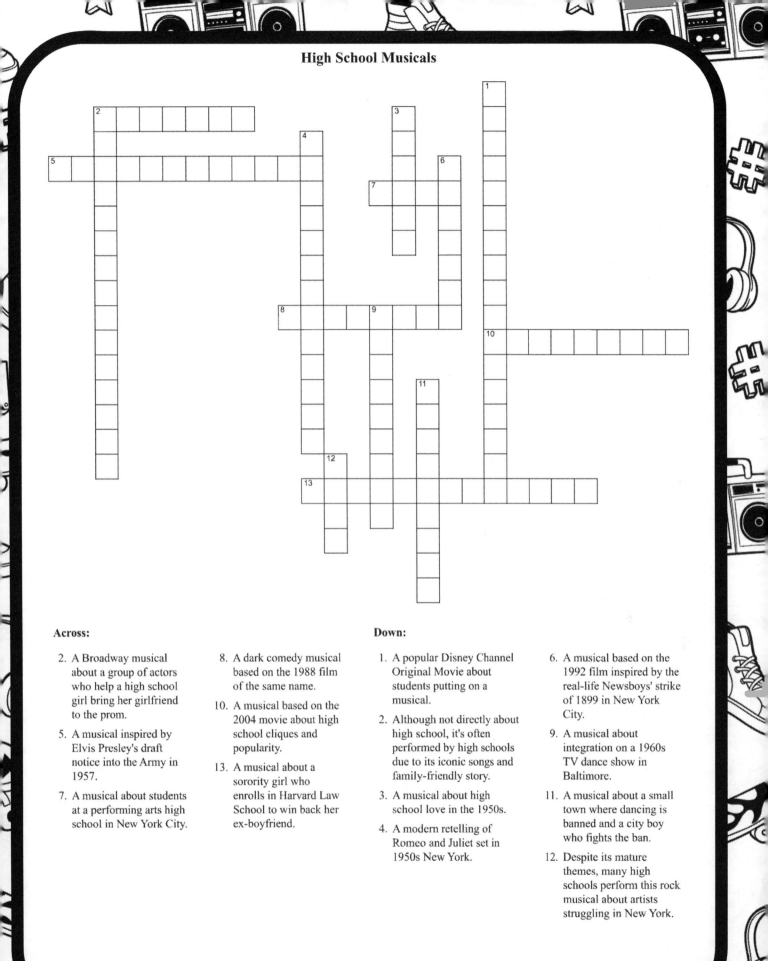

Across:

2. A Broadway musical about a group of actors who help a high school girl bring her girlfriend to the prom.

5. A musical inspired by Elvis Presley's draft notice into the Army in 1957.

7. A musical about students at a performing arts high school in New York City.

8. A dark comedy musical based on the 1988 film of the same name.

10. A musical based on the 2004 movie about high school cliques and popularity.

13. A musical about a sorority girl who enrolls in Harvard Law School to win back her ex-boyfriend.

Down:

1. A popular Disney Channel Original Movie about students putting on a musical.

2. Although not directly about high school, it's often performed by high schools due to its iconic songs and family-friendly story.

3. A musical about high school love in the 1950s.

4. A modern retelling of Romeo and Juliet set in 1950s New York.

6. A musical based on the 1992 film inspired by the real-life Newsboys' strike of 1899 in New York City.

9. A musical about integration on a 1960s TV dance show in Baltimore.

11. A musical about a small town where dancing is banned and a city boy who fights the ban.

12. Despite its mature themes, many high schools perform this rock musical about artists struggling in New York.

Best Friend Tag

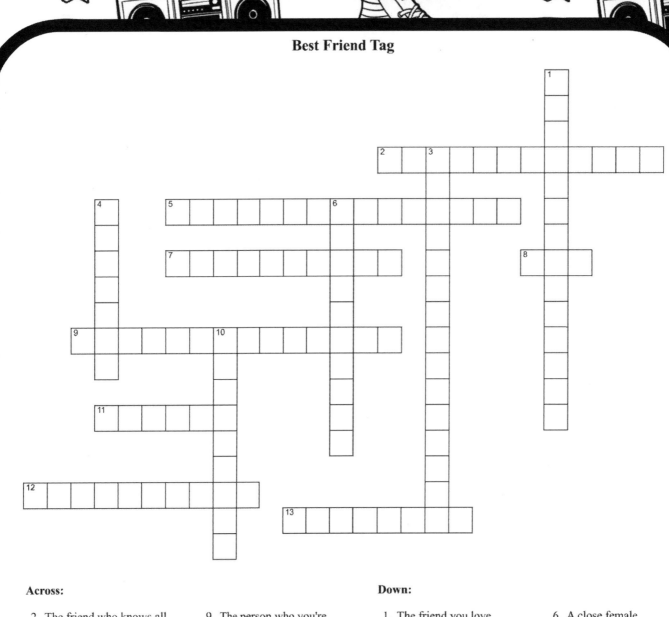

Across:

2. The friend who knows all your secrets.
5. The friend who always gives you the best advice and listens to your problems.
7. A colleague with whom you share a close platonic relationship.
8. A close male friend.
9. The person who you're always getting into trouble with.
11. Your roommate, who often becomes a close friend due to living together.
12. The friend you always study or do homework with.
13. The friend who motivates you to stay fit and accompanies you to the gym.

Down:

1. The friend you love going on adventures and trips with.
3. A friend you've had since your early years.
4. A friend who helps you with social interactions, often in a dating context.
6. A close female friend who feels like a sister.
10. The person who sticks with you through thick and thin.

Food Trends

Across:

3. Increasing consumption of foods derived from plants.

4. Incorporating sea vegetables like kelp and nori into the diet.

6. The versatile vegetable being used as a low-carb substitute in various dishes.

9. A low-carb, high-fat diet that has been popular for weight loss.

10. Non-alcoholic beverages that mimic traditional cocktails.

12. A popular dairy-free milk alternative made from oats.

13. Avoiding foods that contain gluten, a protein found in wheat, barley, and rye.

14. Foods that are nutritionally dense and thus good for one's health, like chia seeds, quinoa, and kale.

Down:

1. The practice of preparing meals ahead of time for convenience and portion control.

2. The use of multifunctional pressure cookers for quick and efficient cooking.

5. Abstaining from the use of animal products, particularly in diet.

7. Consumption of foods like kimchi, sauerkraut, and kefir for their probiotic benefits.

8. Efforts to minimize food waste in all areas.

11. Foods and drinks infused with CBD, a non-psychoactive compound found in cannabis.

Job Interview Tips

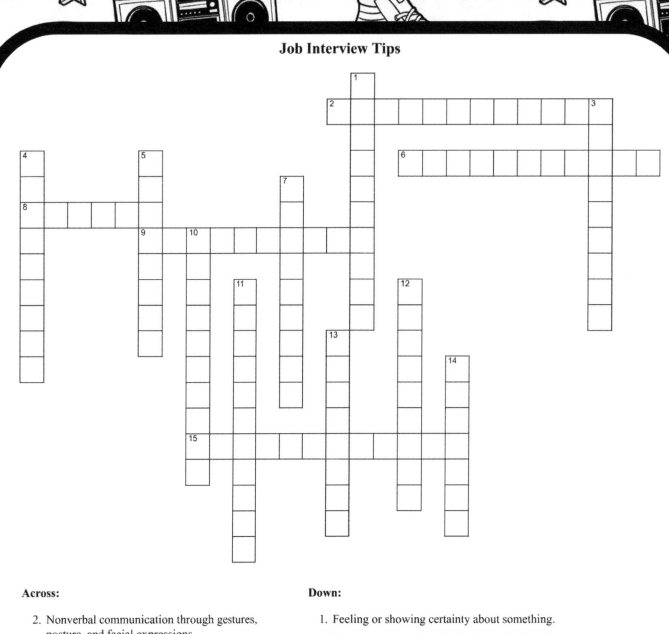

Across:

2. Nonverbal communication through gestures, posture, and facial expressions.

6. The act of making ready or being made ready.

8. The ability to do something well; expertise.

9. The knowledge or skill acquired by a period of practical experience of something.

15. A note of gratitude towards the interviewer for their time.

Down:

1. Feeling or showing certainty about something.

3. The customary code of polite behavior in society or among members of a particular profession or group.

4. The ability to accurately receive and interpret messages in the communication process.

5. To study something thoroughly so as to present in a detailed, accurate manner.

7. A set of rules specifying the garb or type of clothing to be worn by a group or by people under specific circumstances.

10. The practice of being or tendency to be positive or optimistic in attitude.

11. Being on time for the interview.

12. Queries to ask the interviewer about the company and job role.

13. A continuation of something that has already been started.

14. The quality of being honest.

Eco Friendly Brands

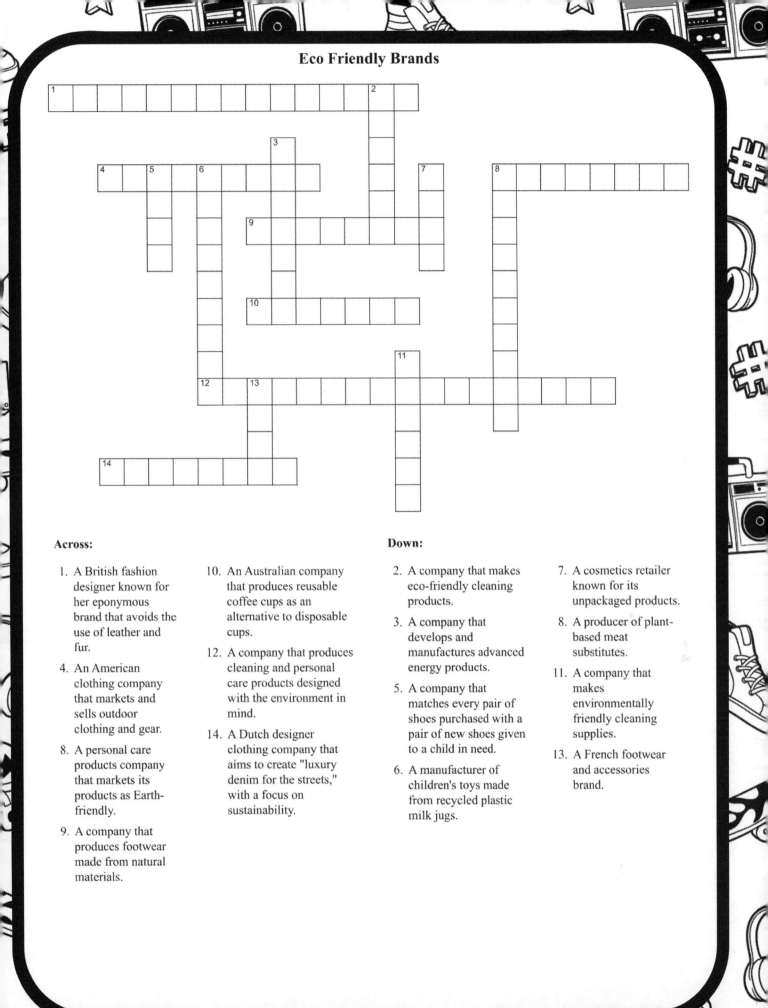

Across:

1. A British fashion designer known for her eponymous brand that avoids the use of leather and fur.

4. An American clothing company that markets and sells outdoor clothing and gear.

8. A personal care products company that markets its products as Earth-friendly.

9. A company that produces footwear made from natural materials.

10. An Australian company that produces reusable coffee cups as an alternative to disposable cups.

12. A company that produces cleaning and personal care products designed with the environment in mind.

14. A Dutch designer clothing company that aims to create "luxury denim for the streets," with a focus on sustainability.

Down:

2. A company that makes eco-friendly cleaning products.

3. A company that develops and manufactures advanced energy products.

5. A company that matches every pair of shoes purchased with a pair of new shoes given to a child in need.

6. A manufacturer of children's toys made from recycled plastic milk jugs.

7. A cosmetics retailer known for its unpackaged products.

8. A producer of plant-based meat substitutes.

11. A company that makes environmentally friendly cleaning supplies.

13. A French footwear and accessories brand.

Dance Styles

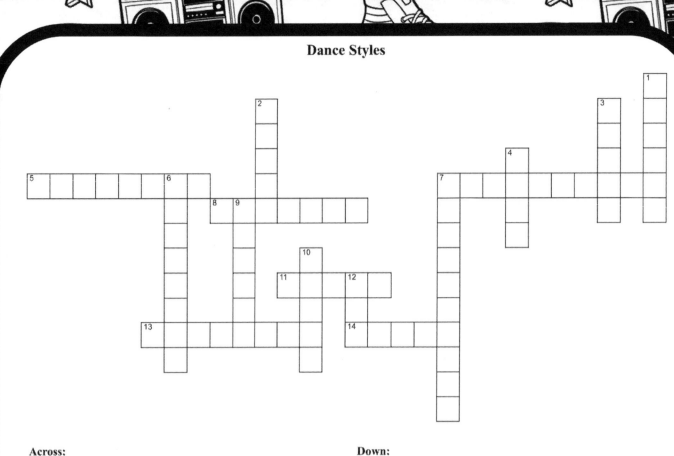

Across:

5. A professionalized art-form based on the folkloric traditions of Southern Spain.

7. Also known as breaking, a street dance style that evolved as part of hip-hop culture.

8. A type of traditional dance from the Indian subcontinent, often in Punjabi musical traditions.

11. A ballroom and folk dance, performed in closed position.

13. A street dance popularized in the United States that is characterized by free, expressive, exaggerated, and highly energetic movement.

14. Originally a Czech dance and genre of dance music familiar throughout Europe and the Americas.

Down:

1. A type of performance dance that originated during the Italian Renaissance in the fifteenth century.

2. A popular form of social dance that originated in New York with strong influences from Latin America.

3. A group of dances that developed with the swing style of jazz music in the 1920s-1940s.

4. A dance style that originated in African-American communities in the early 20th century.

6. A martial art that combines elements of fight, acrobatics, music, dance and rituals in a very elegant and magnetic way.

7. A western-coined name for a traditional Middle Eastern dance.

9. A style of dance that evolved from the hip hop culture.

10. A partner dance and social dance that originated in the 1880s along the Río de la Plata, the natural border between Argentina and Uruguay.

12. A type of dance characterized by using the sounds of metal taps affixed to the heel and toe of shoes striking the floor.

Celebrity Fashion

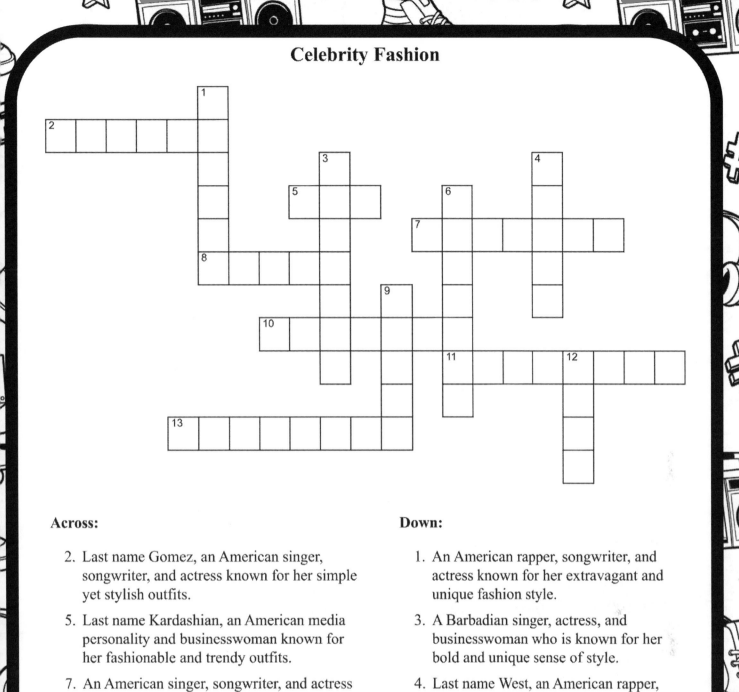

Across:

2. Last name Gomez, an American singer, songwriter, and actress known for her simple yet stylish outfits.

5. Last name Kardashian, an American media personality and businesswoman known for her fashionable and trendy outfits.

7. An American singer, songwriter, and actress known for her glamorous and unique style.

8. Last name Hadid, an American model known for her trendy and stylish outfits.

10. An American actress and singer known for her chic and stylish outfits.

11. An American singer, songwriter, and actress known for her eccentric and bold fashion choices.

13. A Puerto Rican rapper and singer known for his bold and unique fashion style.

Down:

1. An American rapper, songwriter, and actress known for her extravagant and unique fashion style.

3. A Barbadian singer, actress, and businesswoman who is known for her bold and unique sense of style.

4. Last name West, an American rapper, singer, songwriter, record producer, and fashion designer.

6. Last name Jenner, an American model and media personality known for her chic and fashionable style.

9. Last name Styles, an English singer, songwriter, and actor known for his unique and fashionable outfits.

12. Last name Hadid, an American fashion model known for her modern and fashionable outfits.

Young Artists

Across:

6. Last name Mendes, a Canadian singer, songwriter, and model known for hits like "Stitches" and "There's Nothing Holdin' Me Back."

8. Last name Rodrigo, an American singer-songwriter and actress who gained fame with her debut single "drivers license."

9. Last name Gray, an American singer-songwriter and social media personality.

11. An American rapper, singer, and songwriter who rose to fame with his country rap single "Old Town Road."

Down:

1. A stage name of an American singer-songwriter and multi-instrumentalist.

2. Last name Carpenter, an American singer and actress who rose to prominence with her role in the Disney Channel series Girl Meets World.

3. Last name Eilish, an American singer and songwriter who gained fame with her song "Ocean Eyes."

4. A Spanish singer and songwriter who blends flamenco music with urban genres.

5. Last name McRae, a Canadian singer, songwriter, and dancer.

7. An American singer, songwriter, and dancer who was a part of the girl group Fifth Harmony.

10. Last name Lipa, an English singer and songwriter known for songs like "New Rules" and "Don't Start Now."

Streaming Services

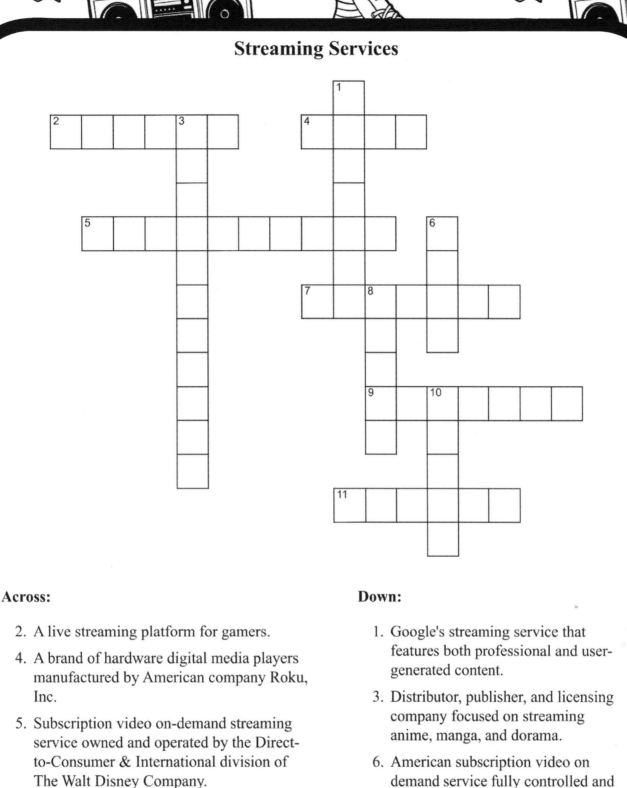

Across:

2. A live streaming platform for gamers.

4. A brand of hardware digital media players manufactured by American company Roku, Inc.

5. Subscription video on-demand streaming service owned and operated by the Direct-to-Consumer & International division of The Walt Disney Company.

7. Provider of streaming movies and TV series.

9. A digital media player and microconsole developed and sold by Apple Inc.

11. Subscription video on demand streaming service from WarnerMedia Entertainment.

Down:

1. Google's streaming service that features both professional and user-generated content.

3. Distributor, publisher, and licensing company focused on streaming anime, manga, and dorama.

6. American subscription video on demand service fully controlled and majority-owned by Walt Disney.

8. Subscription-based music, podcast and video streaming service that combines lossless audio and high-definition music videos.

10. Amazon's paid subscription service that gives access to streaming video, among other benefits.

Youth Sports

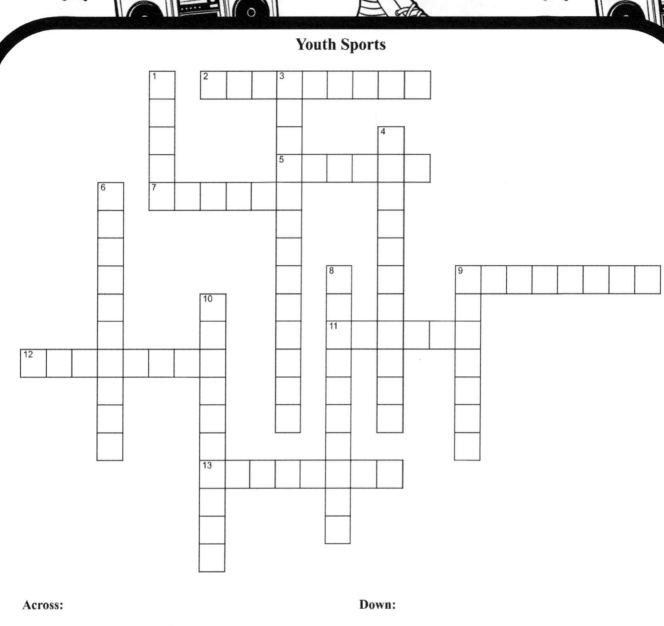

Across:

2. A combat sport involving grappling-type techniques such as clinch fighting, throws and takedowns.

5. A racket sport that can be played individually against a single opponent or between two teams of two players each.

7. A martial art developed in the Ryukyu Kingdom.

9. An individual or team sport that requires to use their entire body to move through water.

11. A popular sport worldwide, also known as football in many countries.

12. Known as American football in other countries, teams try to advance the ball down the field to score points.

13. A sport popular in America, played with a bat and ball.

Down:

1. A sport which includes athletic contests established on the skills of running, jumping, and throwing.

3. An action sport that involves riding and performing tricks using a skateboard.

4. A team game of the hockey family, played on grass or artificial turf.

6. A sport that includes exercises requiring balance, strength, flexibility, agility, coordination, and endurance.

8. A team sport where two teams, usually of five players each, try to score by shooting a ball through a hoop.

9. A surface water sport in which the wave rider, rides on the forward or face of a moving wave.

10. A team sport where teams use their hands to bat a ball back and forth over a high net.

Book Series

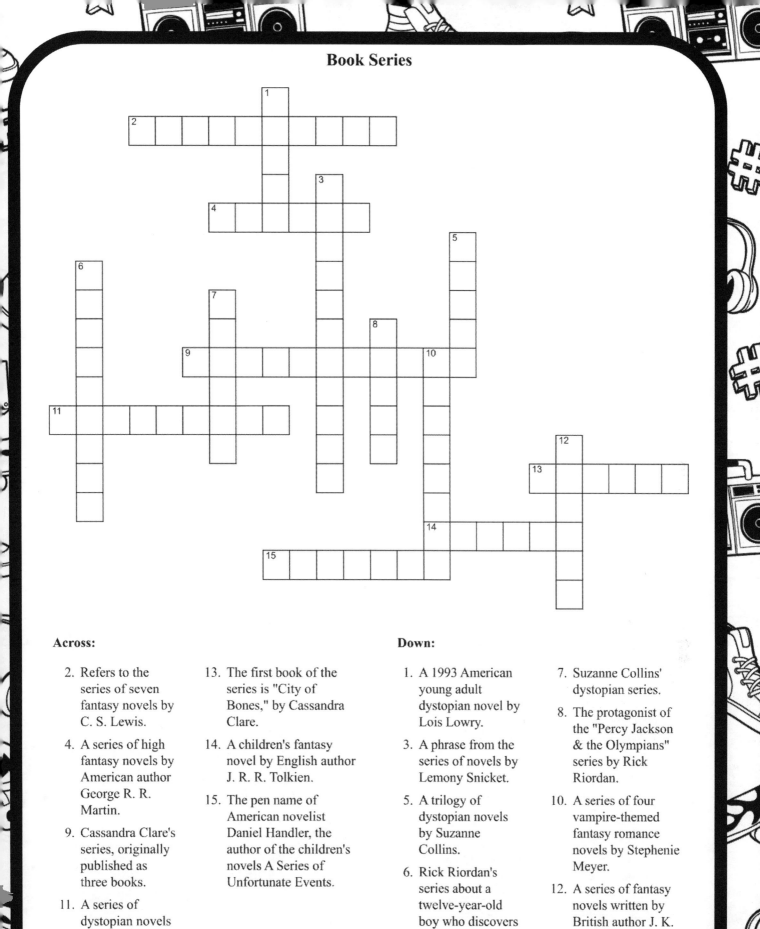

Across:

2. Refers to the series of seven fantasy novels by C. S. Lewis.

4. A series of high fantasy novels by American author George R. R. Martin.

9. Cassandra Clare's series, originally published as three books.

11. A series of dystopian novels by Veronica Roth.

13. The first book of the series is "City of Bones," by Cassandra Clare.

14. A children's fantasy novel by English author J. R. R. Tolkien.

15. The pen name of American novelist Daniel Handler, the author of the children's novels A Series of Unfortunate Events.

Down:

1. A 1993 American young adult dystopian novel by Lois Lowry.

3. A phrase from the series of novels by Lemony Snicket.

5. A trilogy of dystopian novels by Suzanne Collins.

6. Rick Riordan's series about a twelve-year-old boy who discovers he's the son of Poseidon.

7. Suzanne Collins' dystopian series.

8. The protagonist of the "Percy Jackson & the Olympians" series by Rick Riordan.

10. A series of four vampire-themed fantasy romance novels by Stephenie Meyer.

12. A series of fantasy novels written by British author J. K. Rowling.

Social Justice Terms

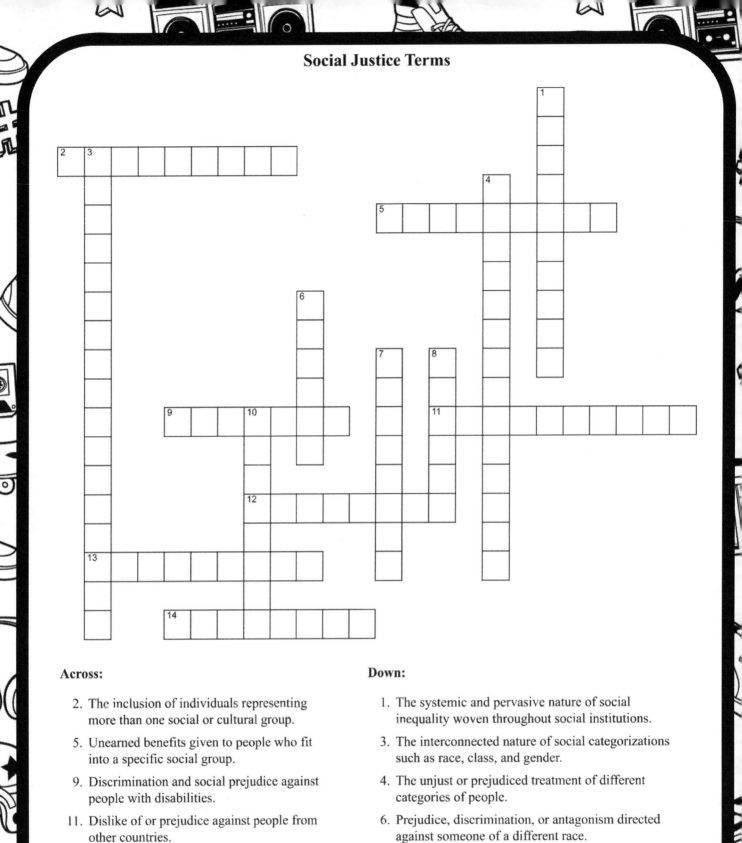

Across:

2. The inclusion of individuals representing more than one social or cultural group.

5. Unearned benefits given to people who fit into a specific social group.

9. Discrimination and social prejudice against people with disabilities.

11. Dislike of or prejudice against people from other countries.

12. The use of vigorous campaigning to bring about social or political change.

13. The action or state of including or being included within a group or structure.

14. The practice of emphasizing social justice, inclusion, and human rights.

Down:

1. The systemic and pervasive nature of social inequality woven throughout social institutions.

3. The interconnected nature of social categorizations such as race, class, and gender.

4. The unjust or prejudiced treatment of different categories of people.

6. Prejudice, discrimination, or antagonism directed against someone of a different race.

7. The advocacy of women's rights on the grounds of political, social, and economic equality to men.

8. Prejudice, stereotyping, or discrimination on the basis of sex.

10. All individuals being treated with the same level of respect and fairness.

Mobile Games

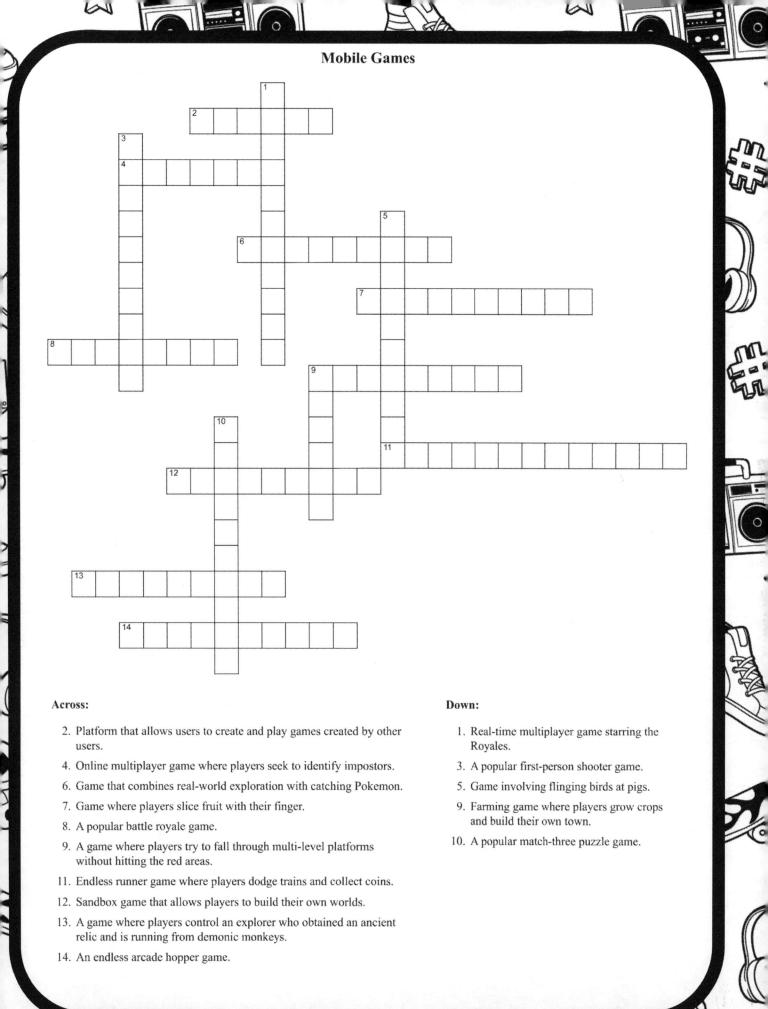

Across:

2. Platform that allows users to create and play games created by other users.

4. Online multiplayer game where players seek to identify impostors.

6. Game that combines real-world exploration with catching Pokemon.

7. Game where players slice fruit with their finger.

8. A popular battle royale game.

9. A game where players try to fall through multi-level platforms without hitting the red areas.

11. Endless runner game where players dodge trains and collect coins.

12. Sandbox game that allows players to build their own worlds.

13. A game where players control an explorer who obtained an ancient relic and is running from demonic monkeys.

14. An endless arcade hopper game.

Down:

1. Real-time multiplayer game starring the Royales.

3. A popular first-person shooter game.

5. Game involving flinging birds at pigs.

9. Farming game where players grow crops and build their own town.

10. A popular match-three puzzle game.

Young Adult Authors

Across:

1. Known for books like "Speak".

4. Author of "The Mortal Instruments" series.

5. Author of the "Divergent" series.

7. Author of "Simon vs. the Homo Sapiens Agenda".

9. Author of "The Maze Runner" series.

13. Author of the "Hunger Games" series.

14. Author of "All the Bright Places".

Down:

2. Author of the "Percy Jackson" series.

3. Author of "The Wrath & the Dawn" duology.

6. Author of "The Fault in Our Stars".

8. Author of the "To All the Boys I've Loved Before" series.

10. Author of the "Harry Potter" series.

11. Pseudonym of the author of "A Series of Unfortunate Events".

12. Author of "Everything, Everything".

Study Abroad Destinations

Across:

1. Rich in culture and history.
4. Home to the city of love, Paris.
5. Home to art, history, and pizza.
9. Offers high quality education and a unique culture.
10. Known for its friendly locals and beautiful landscapes.
11. Known for its historic cities and beautiful beaches.
12. Offers a mix of tradition and modernity.

Down:

2. Rapidly growing, with a unique blend of ancient and modern culture.
3. Offers diverse culture and beautiful landscapes.
6. Known for its wildlife and outdoor adventures.
7. Known for its friendly locals and green countryside.
8. Known for its rich history and education system.

Extracurricular Activities

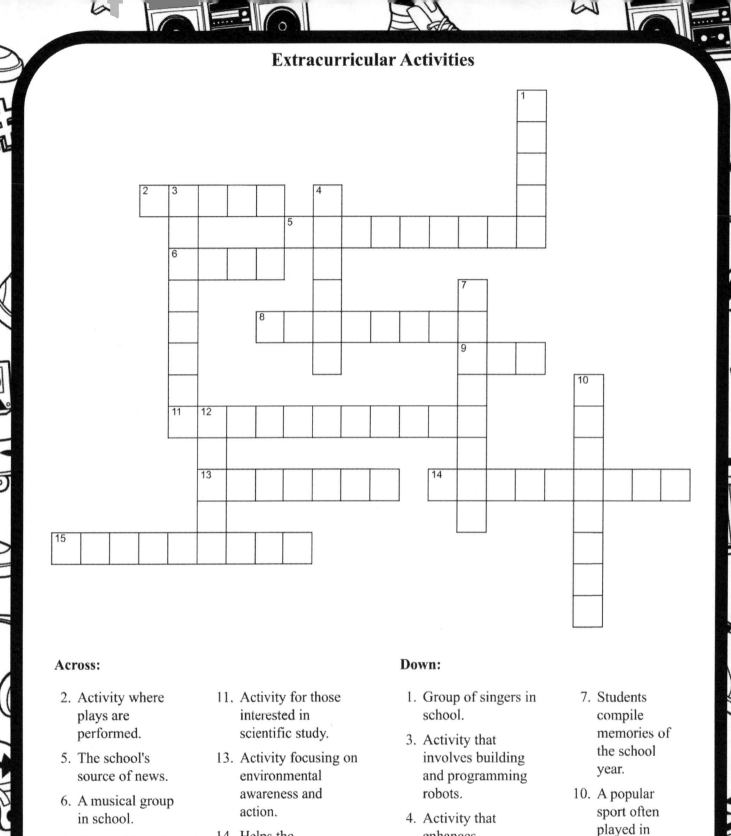

Across:

2. Activity where plays are performed.

5. The school's source of news.

6. A musical group in school.

8. Competitions for those who excel in mathematics.

9. Activity that involves drawing, painting, and creating.

11. Activity for those interested in scientific study.

13. Activity focusing on environmental awareness and action.

14. Helps the community through service.

15. Group of instrumentalists in school.

Down:

1. Group of singers in school.

3. Activity that involves building and programming robots.

4. Activity that enhances argumentative and public speaking skills.

7. Students compile memories of the school year.

10. A popular sport often played in schools.

12. A board game that develops strategic thinking.

Teen Idols

Across:

3. English actress known for her role as Eleven in "Stranger Things".

6. She got her start on "Barney & Friends" and later starred in "Wizards of Waverly Place".

7. American singer-songwriter known for narrative songwriting.

10. Singer known for her hits like "Firework" and "Roar".

12. Singer who began her career in the Broadway musical 13.

13. Former One Direction member known for his solo career.

14. English actor known for playing Spider-Man in the Marvel Cinematic Universe.

Down:

1. Actress known for her role in the series "Girl Meets World".

2. Canadian singer-songwriter known for his hits like "Stitches".

4. One of the most popular models in the world.

5. Canadian singer who got his start on YouTube.

8. Star of Disney Channel's "Hannah Montana".

9. One of the members of the pop rock band the Jonas Brothers.

11. Actress known for her roles in "Euphoria" and "Spider-Man".

Fantasy Creatures

Across:

1. A monstrous creature from European folklore.

8. A mythical sea creature with the upper body of a human and the tail of a fish.

10. A creature with the upper body of a human and the lower body of a horse.

11. A human with the ability to shapeshift into a wolf.

12. A supernatural being in Germanic mythology and folklore.

13. A large, serpent-like legendary creature.

Down:

2. A female spirit in Irish mythology who heralds the death of a family member.

3. A type of mythical being or legendary creature in European folklore.

4. A creature from folklore that subsists by feeding on the vital essence of the living.

5. A mythical creature with a single large, pointed, spiraling horn.

6. A mythical creature portrayed in Classical times with the head and tail of a bull and the body of a man.

7. A mythical creature with the body of a lion and the head and wings of an eagle.

9. A long-lived bird that cyclically regenerates or is born again.

Graphic Novels

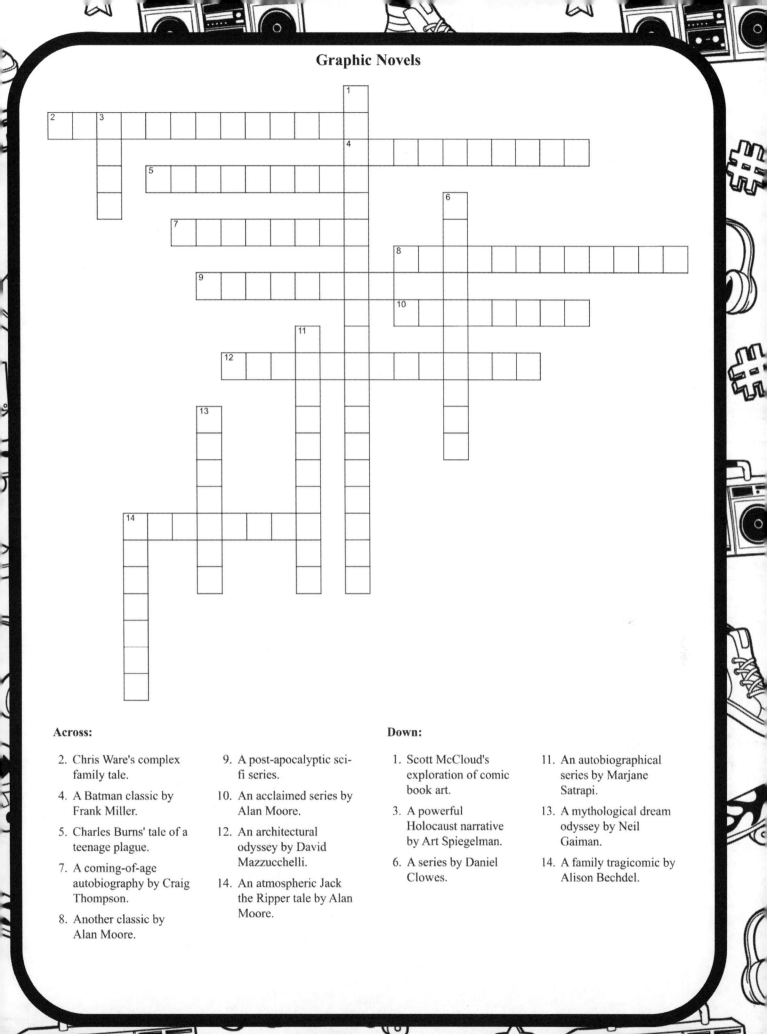

Across:

2. Chris Ware's complex family tale.

4. A Batman classic by Frank Miller.

5. Charles Burns' tale of a teenage plague.

7. A coming-of-age autobiography by Craig Thompson.

8. Another classic by Alan Moore.

9. A post-apocalyptic sci-fi series.

10. An acclaimed series by Alan Moore.

12. An architectural odyssey by David Mazzucchelli.

14. An atmospheric Jack the Ripper tale by Alan Moore.

Down:

1. Scott McCloud's exploration of comic book art.

3. A powerful Holocaust narrative by Art Spiegelman.

6. A series by Daniel Clowes.

11. An autobiographical series by Marjane Satrapi.

13. A mythological dream odyssey by Neil Gaiman.

14. A family tragicomic by Alison Bechdel.

Study Techniques

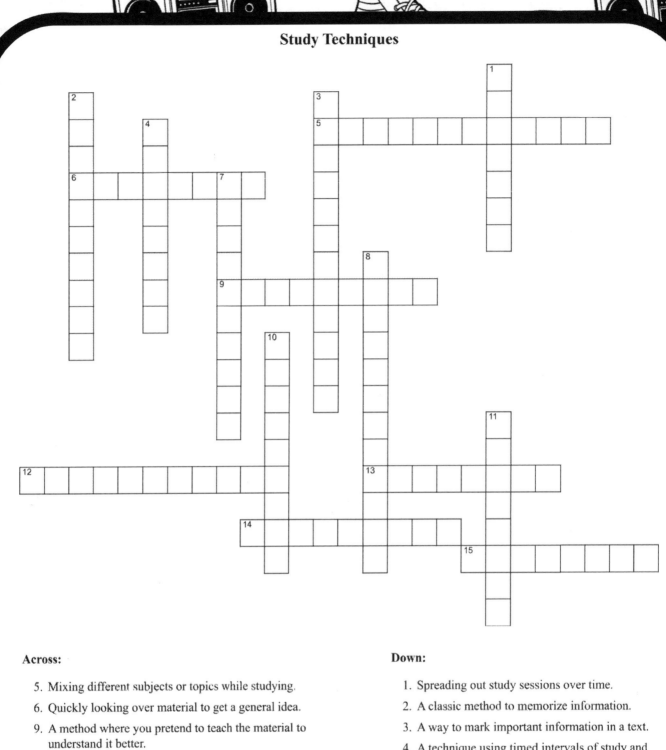

Across:

5. Mixing different subjects or topics while studying.
6. Quickly looking over material to get a general idea.
9. A method where you pretend to teach the material to understand it better.
12. Explaining the subject in detail.
13. Testing your own knowledge before the actual exam.
14. Memory techniques using systems like acronyms or visualizations.
15. Graphical way to represent ideas and concepts.

Down:

1. Spreading out study sessions over time.
2. A classic method to memorize information.
3. A way to mark important information in a text.
4. A technique using timed intervals of study and breaks.
7. A fundamental skill for any student.
8. Rewriting the information in your own words.
10. Making a summary of the main points.
11. Breaking down information into bite-sized pieces.

Popular Podcasts

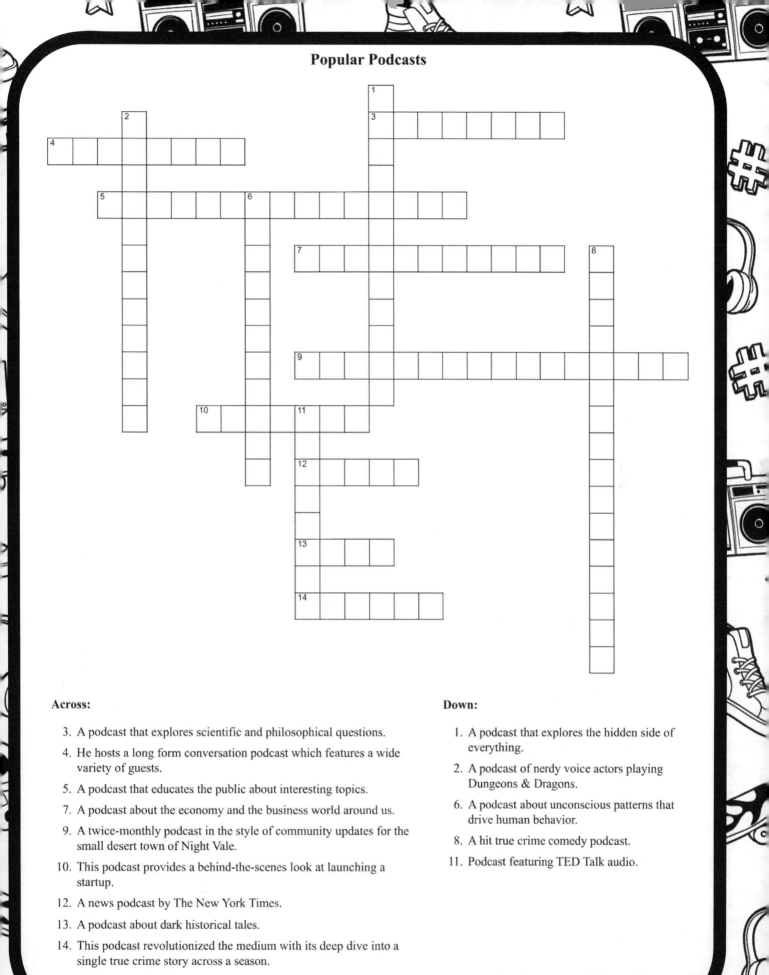

Across:

3. A podcast that explores scientific and philosophical questions.
4. He hosts a long form conversation podcast which features a wide variety of guests.
5. A podcast that educates the public about interesting topics.
7. A podcast about the economy and the business world around us.
9. A twice-monthly podcast in the style of community updates for the small desert town of Night Vale.
10. This podcast provides a behind-the-scenes look at launching a startup.
12. A news podcast by The New York Times.
13. A podcast about dark historical tales.
14. This podcast revolutionized the medium with its deep dive into a single true crime story across a season.

Down:

1. A podcast that explores the hidden side of everything.
2. A podcast of nerdy voice actors playing Dungeons & Dragons.
6. A podcast about unconscious patterns that drive human behavior.
8. A hit true crime comedy podcast.
11. Podcast featuring TED Talk audio.

Science Fiction Books

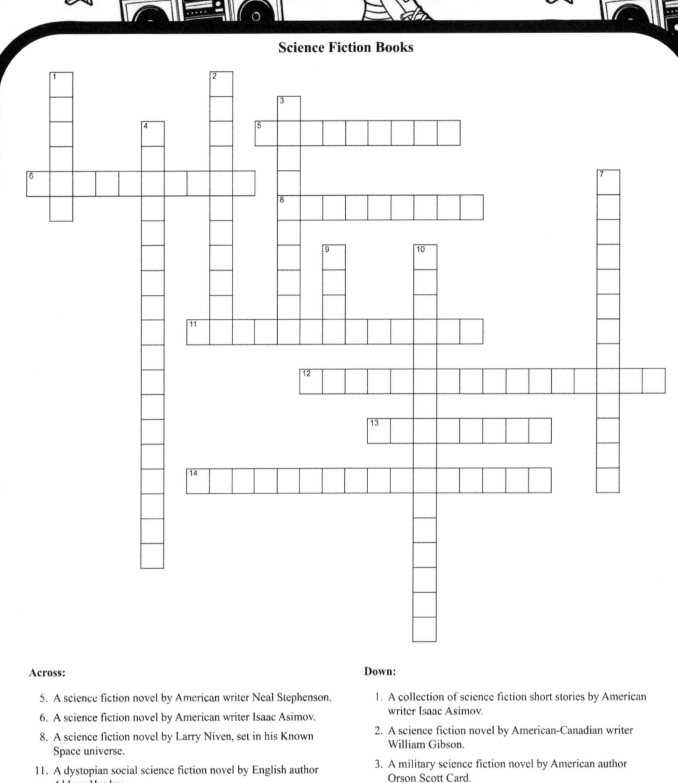

Across:

5. A science fiction novel by American writer Neal Stephenson.

6. A science fiction novel by American writer Isaac Asimov.

8. A science fiction novel by Larry Niven, set in his Known Space universe.

11. A dystopian social science fiction novel by English author Aldous Huxley.

12. A comedic science fiction series written by Douglas Adams.

13. A Hugo Award-winning science fiction novel by American writer Dan Simmons.

14. A science fiction novel by U.S. writer Ursula K. Le Guin.

Down:

1. A collection of science fiction short stories by American writer Isaac Asimov.

2. A science fiction novel by American-Canadian writer William Gibson.

3. A military science fiction novel by American author Orson Scott Card.

4. A science fiction-infused anti-war novel by Kurt Vonnegut.

7. A dystopian novel by American writer Ray Bradbury.

9. A science fiction novel by American author Frank Herbert.

10. A military science fiction novel by American writer Robert A. Heinlein.

Young Entrepreneurs

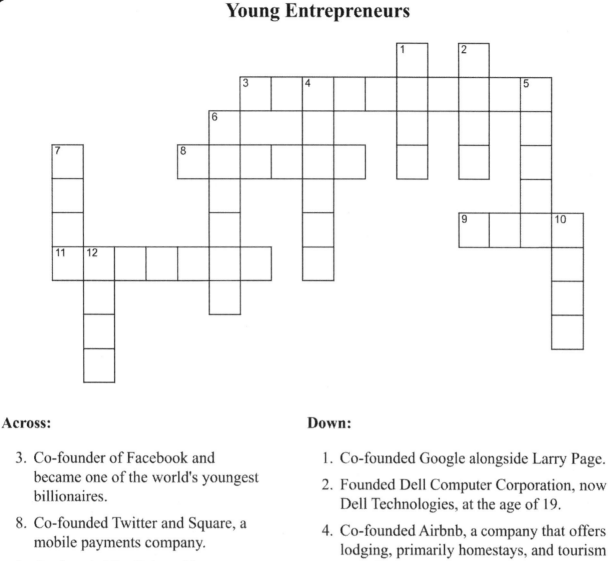

Across:

3. Co-founder of Facebook and became one of the world's youngest billionaires.

8. Co-founded Twitter and Square, a mobile payments company.

9. Co-founded PayPal, and later founded SpaceX and became CEO of Tesla.

11. Co-founder and CEO of the American social media company Snap Inc.

Down:

1. Co-founded Google alongside Larry Page.

2. Founded Dell Computer Corporation, now Dell Technologies, at the age of 19.

4. Co-founded Airbnb, a company that offers lodging, primarily homestays, and tourism experiences.

5. Co-founded Microsoft, one of the world's largest personal-computer software companies.

6. Founder and former CEO of Theranos, a now-defunct health technology company.

7. Co-founded Apple Inc., creator of the iPhone.

10. Founded Tumblr, a social networking website, at the age of 21.

12. Co-founded Google, now one of the most visited websites worldwide.

Makeup Brands

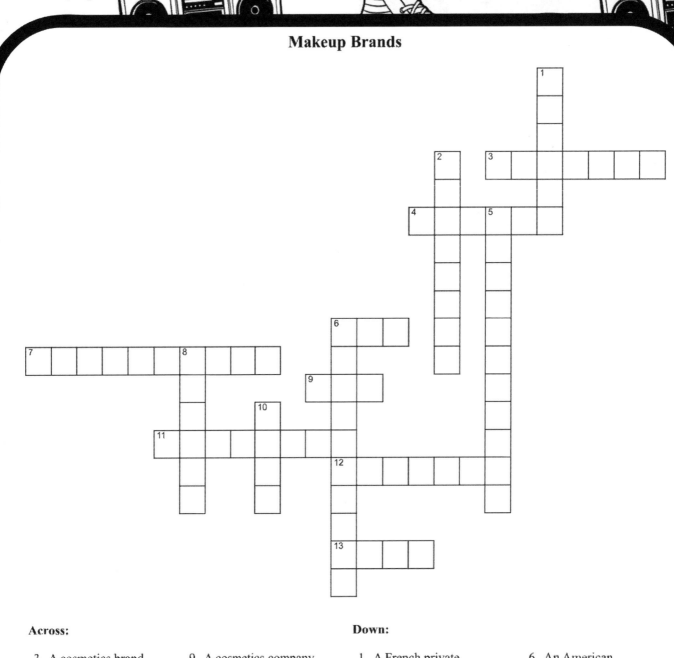

Across:

3. A cosmetics brand selling at over 2,000 shops in more than 30 countries.

4. The world's largest cosmetics company.

6. A cosmetics manufacturer founded in Toronto.

7. An American professional makeup artist and the founder of Bobbi Brown Cosmetics.

9. A cosmetics company that is a subsidiary of L Oréal.

11. A manufacturer of skincare, cosmetics, toiletries, and fragrances.

12. A French luxury perfumes and cosmetics house.

13. A French cosmetics and skincare company founded by make-up artist and photographer François Nars.

Down:

1. A French private company owned by Alain and Gerard Wertheimer, grandsons of Pierre Wertheimer.

2. A cosmetics brand headquartered in Brea, California.

5. A multinational manufacturer and marketer of prestige skincare, makeup, fragrance and hair care products.

6. An American multinational cosmetics, skin care, perfume, and personal care company.

8. An American multinational cosmetics, skin care, fragrance, and personal care company.

10. A French luxury goods company controlled and chaired by French businessman Bernard Arnault.

Tech Startups

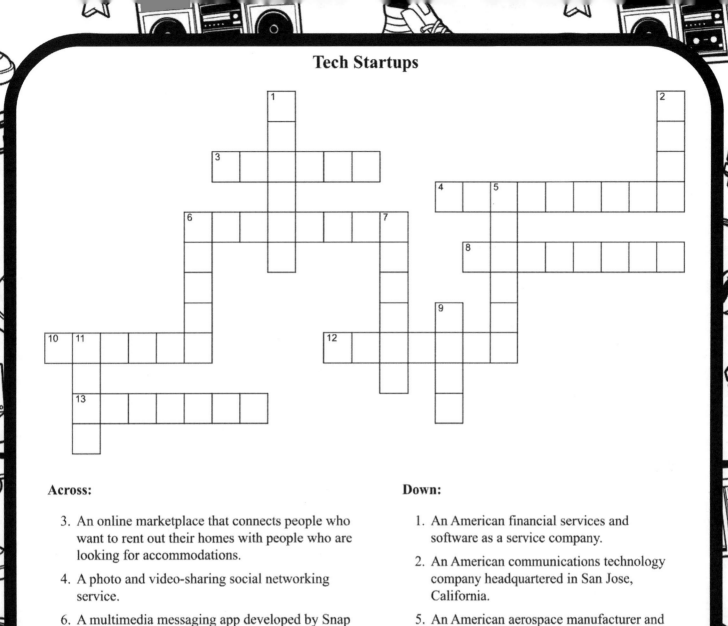

Across:

3. An online marketplace that connects people who want to rent out their homes with people who are looking for accommodations.

4. A photo and video-sharing social networking service.

6. A multimedia messaging app developed by Snap Inc.

8. A public American software company that specializes in big data analytics.

10. An American commercial real estate company that provides shared workspaces.

12. A file hosting service operated by Dropbox, Inc., headquartered in San Francisco, California.

13. A digital music service that gives you access to millions of songs.

Down:

1. An American financial services and software as a service company.

2. An American communications technology company headquartered in San Jose, California.

5. An American aerospace manufacturer and space transportation company founded by Elon Musk.

6. An American cloud-based set of proprietary team collaboration tools and services.

7. A social media platform for creating, sharing, and discovering short videos.

9. A company offering ridesharing, food delivery, package delivery, couriers, freight transportation, and more.

11. An American e-commerce website focused on handmade or vintage items and craft supplies.

Streetwear Brands

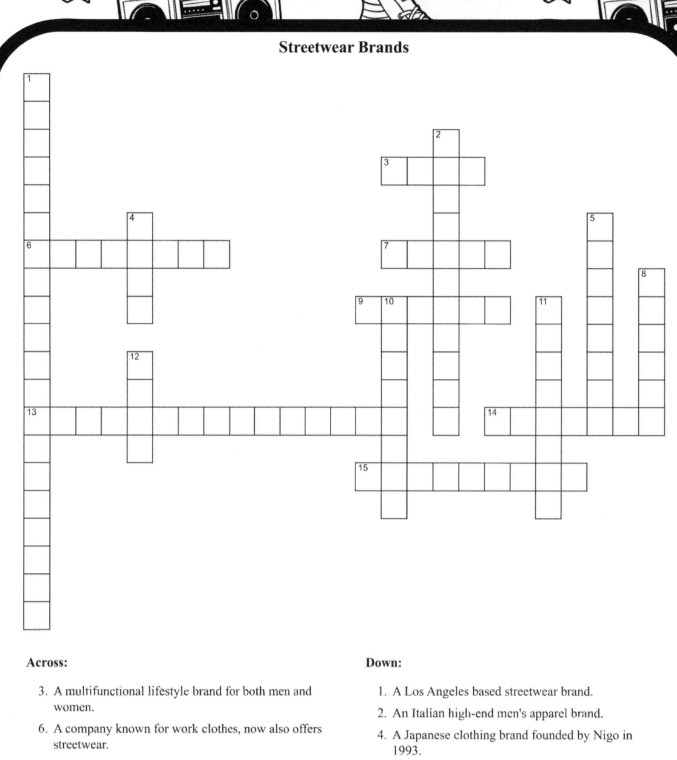

Across:

3. A multifunctional lifestyle brand for both men and women.

6. A company known for work clothes, now also offers streetwear.

7. A brand tied to Kanye West s collaboration with Adidas.

9. A clothing brand started in the early 1980s by Shawn Stussy.

13. A Japanese fashion label headed by Rei Kawakubo.

14. A skateboarding shop and clothing brand established in New York City.

15. A luxury streetwear label founded by Jerry Lorenzo.

Down:

1. A Los Angeles based streetwear brand.

2. An Italian high-end men's apparel brand.

4. A Japanese clothing brand founded by Nigo in 1993.

5. A luxury fashion label founded by American designer Virgil Abloh.

8. A British skateboarding shop and clothing brand.

10. A skateboarding magazine and clothing brand.

11. An American manufacturer of clothing, specializing in sportswear.

12. A clothing company founded by artist Shepard Fairey.

Concert Venues

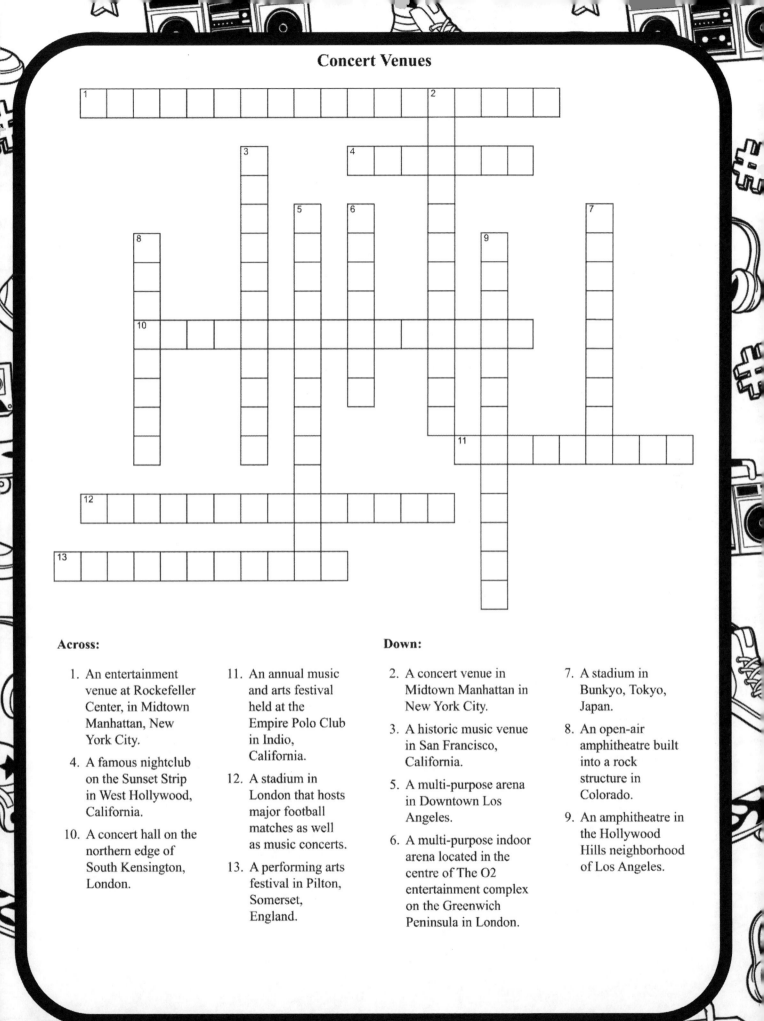

Across:

1. An entertainment venue at Rockefeller Center, in Midtown Manhattan, New York City.

4. A famous nightclub on the Sunset Strip in West Hollywood, California.

10. A concert hall on the northern edge of South Kensington, London.

11. An annual music and arts festival held at the Empire Polo Club in Indio, California.

12. A stadium in London that hosts major football matches as well as music concerts.

13. A performing arts festival in Pilton, Somerset, England.

Down:

2. A concert venue in Midtown Manhattan in New York City.

3. A historic music venue in San Francisco, California.

5. A multi-purpose arena in Downtown Los Angeles.

6. A multi-purpose indoor arena located in the centre of The O2 entertainment complex on the Greenwich Peninsula in London.

7. A stadium in Bunkyo, Tokyo, Japan.

8. An open-air amphitheatre built into a rock structure in Colorado.

9. An amphitheatre in the Hollywood Hills neighborhood of Los Angeles.

Band Members

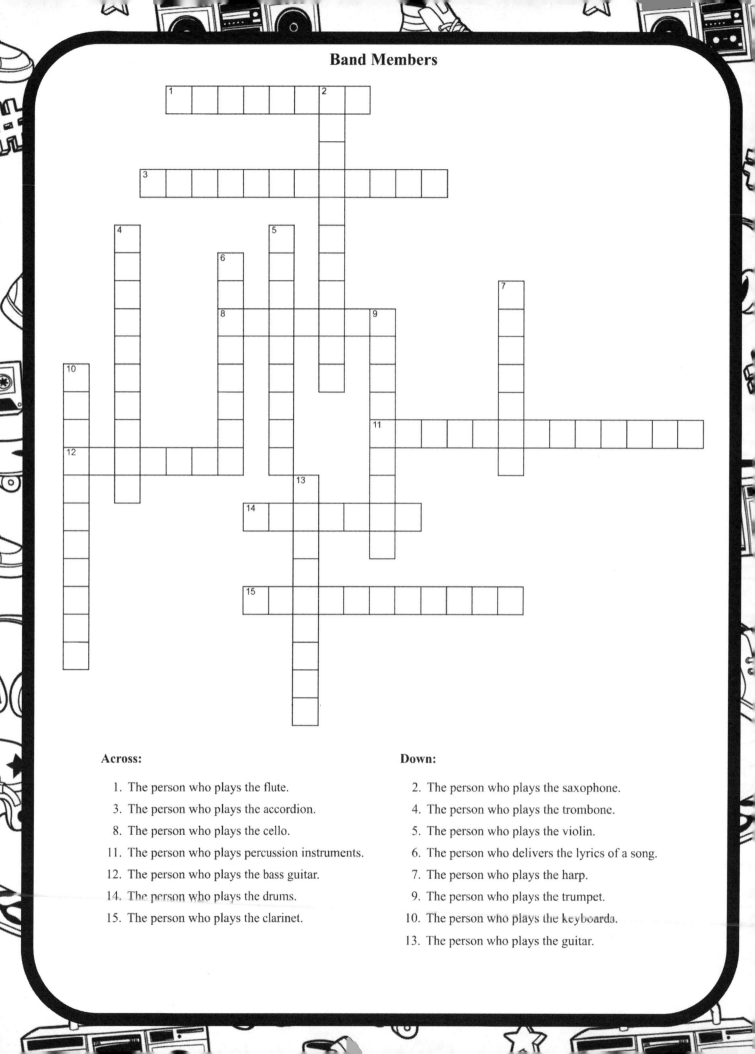

Across:

1. The person who plays the flute.
3. The person who plays the accordion.
8. The person who plays the cello.
11. The person who plays percussion instruments.
12. The person who plays the bass guitar.
14. The person who plays the drums.
15. The person who plays the clarinet.

Down:

2. The person who plays the saxophone.
4. The person who plays the trombone.
5. The person who plays the violin.
6. The person who delivers the lyrics of a song.
7. The person who plays the harp.
9. The person who plays the trumpet.
10. The person who plays the keyboards.
13. The person who plays the guitar.

Musica lInstruments

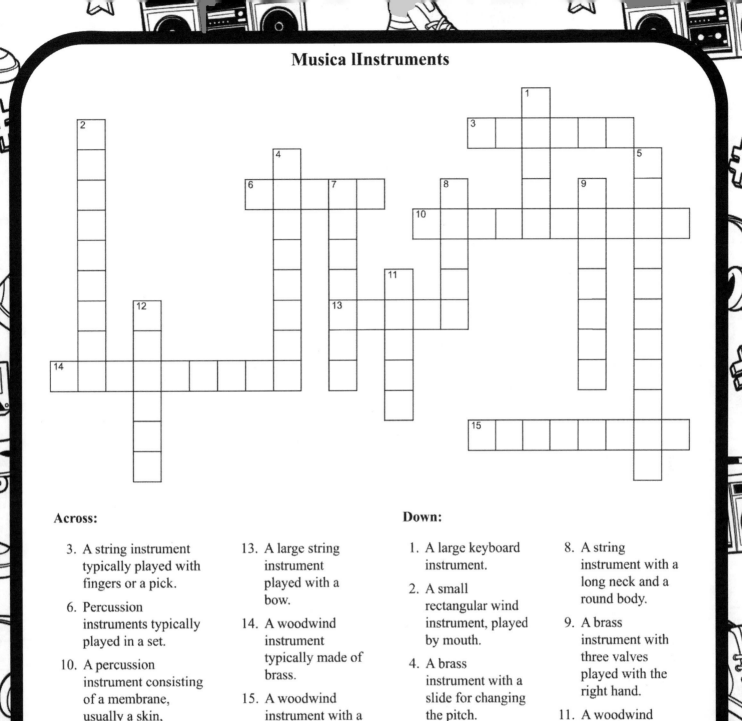

Across:

3. A string instrument typically played with fingers or a pick.

6. Percussion instruments typically played in a set.

10. A percussion instrument consisting of a membrane, usually a skin, stretched over a circular frame.

13. A large string instrument played with a bow.

14. A woodwind instrument typically made of brass.

15. A woodwind instrument with a single-reed mouthpiece.

Down:

1. A large keyboard instrument.

2. A small rectangular wind instrument, played by mouth.

4. A brass instrument with a slide for changing the pitch.

5. An electronic musical instrument, typically operated by a keyboard.

7. A pair of small short-handled rattles.

8. A string instrument with a long neck and a round body.

9. A brass instrument with three valves played with the right hand.

11. A woodwind instrument played by blowing air across the opening.

12. A string instrument played with a bow.

Health Foods

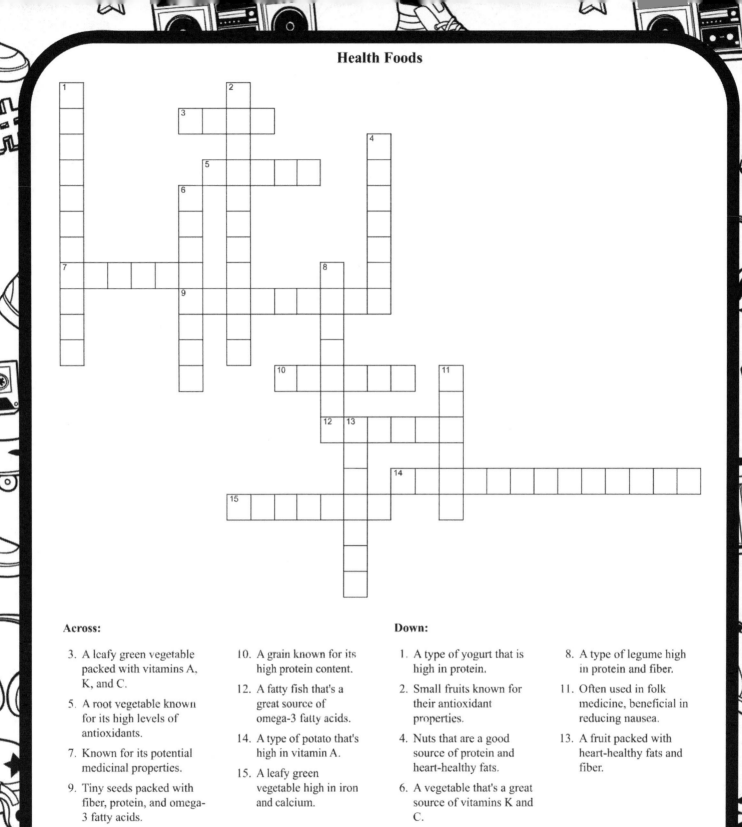

Across:

3. A leafy green vegetable packed with vitamins A, K, and C.

5. A root vegetable known for its high levels of antioxidants.

7. Known for its potential medicinal properties.

9. Tiny seeds packed with fiber, protein, and omega-3 fatty acids.

10. A grain known for its high protein content.

12. A fatty fish that's a great source of omega-3 fatty acids.

14. A type of potato that's high in vitamin A.

15. A leafy green vegetable high in iron and calcium.

Down:

1. A type of yogurt that is high in protein.

2. Small fruits known for their antioxidant properties.

4. Nuts that are a good source of protein and heart-healthy fats.

6. A vegetable that's a great source of vitamins K and C.

8. A type of legume high in protein and fiber.

11. Often used in folk medicine, beneficial in reducing nausea.

13. A fruit packed with heart-healthy fats and fiber.

Reality TV Shows

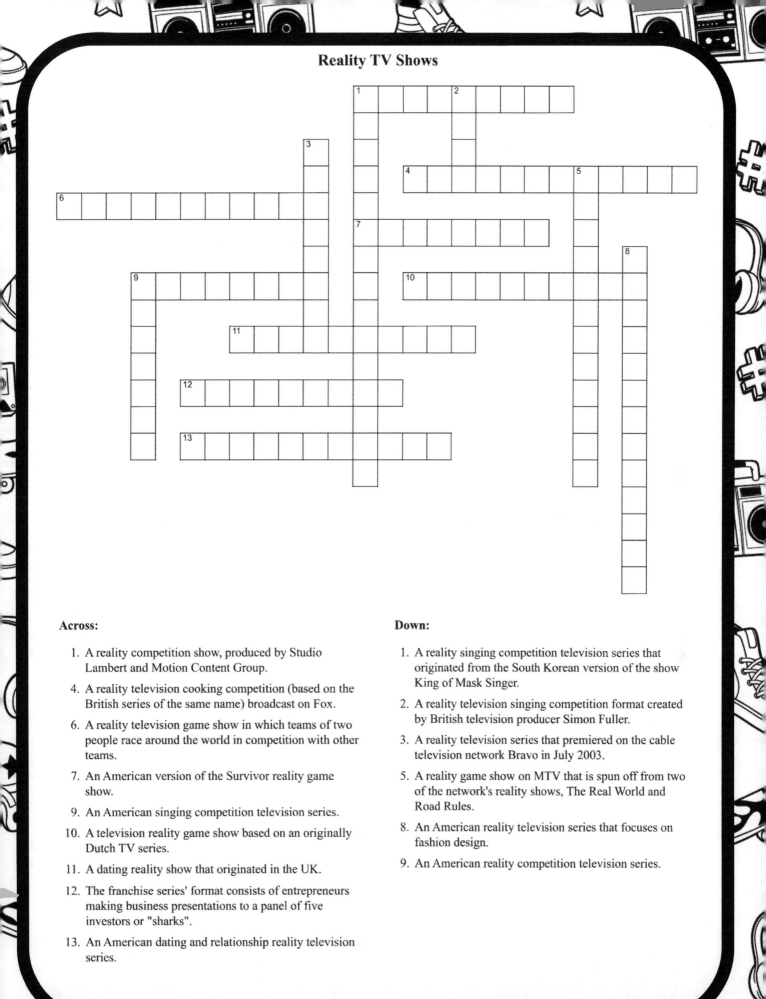

Across:

1. A reality competition show, produced by Studio Lambert and Motion Content Group.

4. A reality television cooking competition (based on the British series of the same name) broadcast on Fox.

6. A reality television game show in which teams of two people race around the world in competition with other teams.

7. An American version of the Survivor reality game show.

9. An American singing competition television series.

10. A television reality game show based on an originally Dutch TV series.

11. A dating reality show that originated in the UK.

12. The franchise series' format consists of entrepreneurs making business presentations to a panel of five investors or "sharks".

13. An American dating and relationship reality television series.

Down:

1. A reality singing competition television series that originated from the South Korean version of the show King of Mask Singer.

2. A reality television singing competition format created by British television producer Simon Fuller.

3. A reality television series that premiered on the cable television network Bravo in July 2003.

5. A reality game show on MTV that is spun off from two of the network's reality shows, The Real World and Road Rules.

8. An American reality television series that focuses on fashion design.

9. An American reality competition television series.

Skate Brands

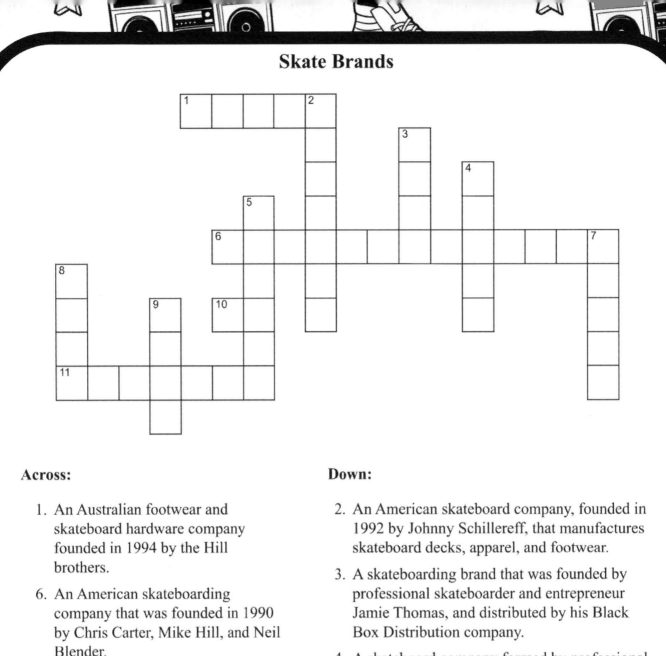

Across:

1. An Australian footwear and skateboard hardware company founded in 1994 by the Hill brothers.

6. An American skateboarding company that was founded in 1990 by Chris Carter, Mike Hill, and Neil Blender.

10. An American company that specializes in footwear for action sports, including skateboarding and snowboarding.

11. An American skateboarding shop and clothing brand established in New York City in April 1994.

Down:

2. An American skateboard company, founded in 1992 by Johnny Schillereff, that manufactures skateboard decks, apparel, and footwear.

3. A skateboarding brand that was founded by professional skateboarder and entrepreneur Jamie Thomas, and distributed by his Black Box Distribution company.

4. A skateboard company formed by professional skateboarder Andrew Reynolds and creative founder Jay Strickland in 2000.

5. A now defunct skateboard company founded in Lyon, France in 1997 by Jeremie Daclin.

7. A skateboarding team that was initially formed by Mike Ternasky in 1991.

8. An American manufacturer of skateboarding shoes and related apparel, based in Santa Ana, California.

9. A skateboard company based in Torrance, California.

Festivals

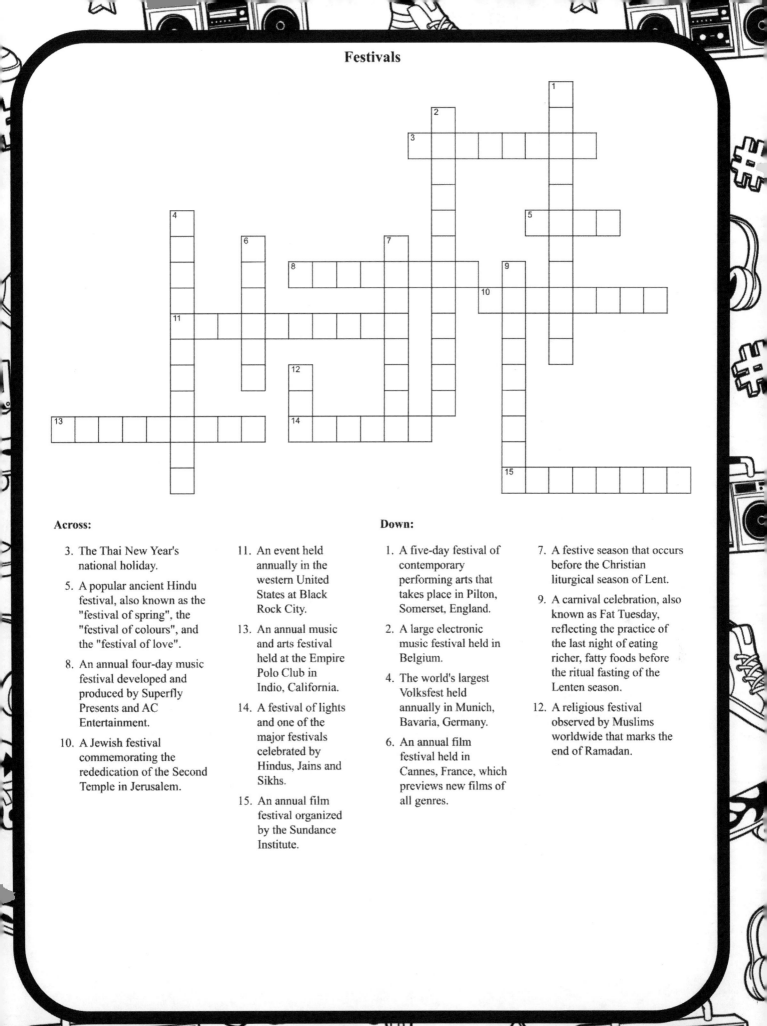

Across:

3. The Thai New Year's national holiday.

5. A popular ancient Hindu festival, also known as the "festival of spring", the "festival of colours", and the "festival of love".

8. An annual four-day music festival developed and produced by Superfly Presents and AC Entertainment.

10. A Jewish festival commemorating the rededication of the Second Temple in Jerusalem.

11. An event held annually in the western United States at Black Rock City.

13. An annual music and arts festival held at the Empire Polo Club in Indio, California.

14. A festival of lights and one of the major festivals celebrated by Hindus, Jains and Sikhs.

15. An annual film festival organized by the Sundance Institute.

Down:

1. A five-day festival of contemporary performing arts that takes place in Pilton, Somerset, England.

2. A large electronic music festival held in Belgium.

4. The world's largest Volksfest held annually in Munich, Bavaria, Germany.

6. An annual film festival held in Cannes, France, which previews new films of all genres.

7. A festive season that occurs before the Christian liturgical season of Lent.

9. A carnival celebration, also known as Fat Tuesday, reflecting the practice of the last night of eating richer, fatty foods before the ritual fasting of the Lenten season.

12. A religious festival observed by Muslims worldwide that marks the end of Ramadan.

Backpacking Destinations

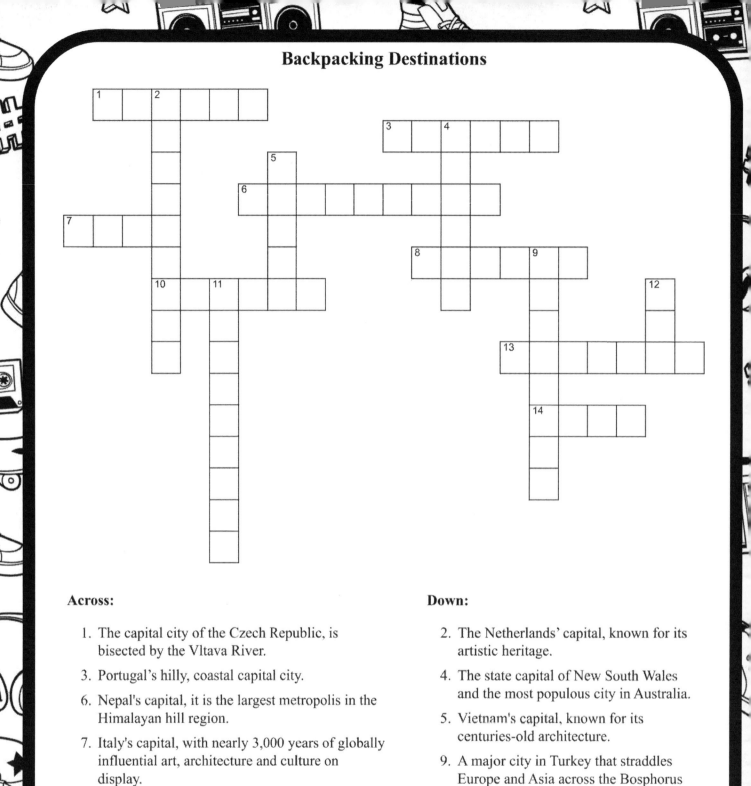

Across:

1. The capital city of the Czech Republic, is bisected by the Vltava River.

3. Portugal's hilly, coastal capital city.

6. Nepal's capital, it is the largest metropolis in the Himalayan hill region.

7. Italy's capital, with nearly 3,000 years of globally influential art, architecture and culture on display.

8. Germany's capital, known for its art scene and modern landmarks.

10. The capital of and largest city in Ireland.

13. Thailand's capital, a large city known for ornate shrines and vibrant street life.

14. An Indonesian island known for its forested volcanic mountains, iconic rice paddies, beaches and coral reefs.

Down:

2. The Netherlands' capital, known for its artistic heritage.

4. The state capital of New South Wales and the most populous city in Australia.

5. Vietnam's capital, known for its centuries-old architecture.

9. A major city in Turkey that straddles Europe and Asia across the Bosphorus Strait.

11. The cosmopolitan capital of Spain's Catalonia region.

12. A huge seaside city in Brazil, famed for its Copacabana and Ipanema beaches.

Hobbies

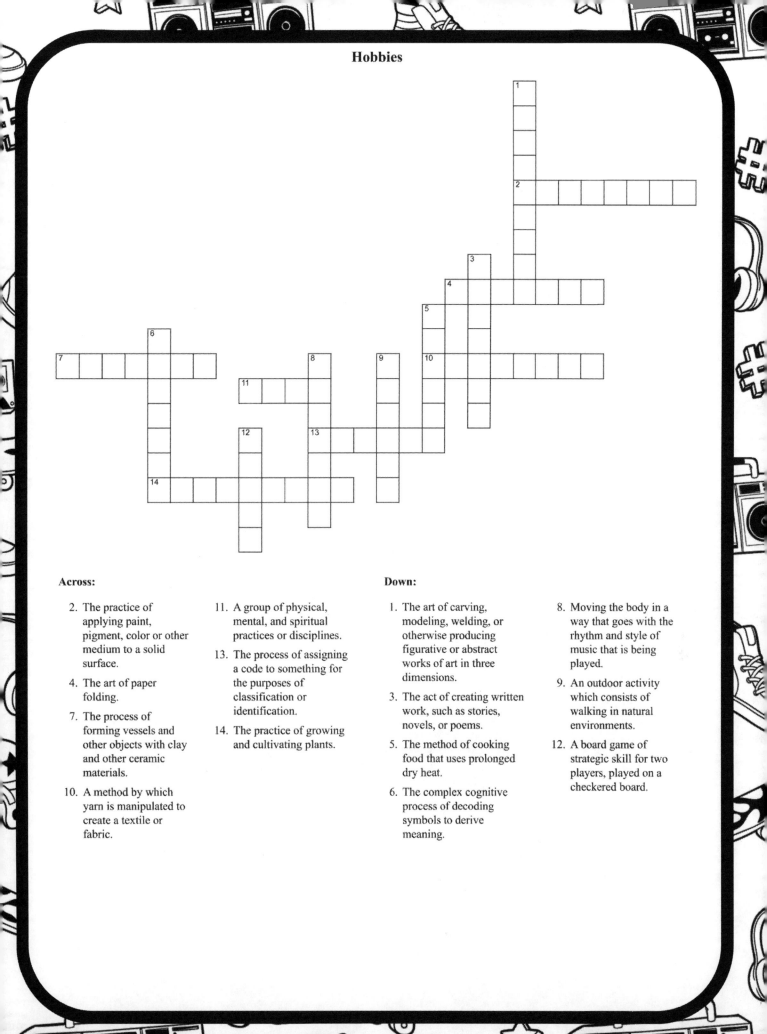

Across:

2. The practice of applying paint, pigment, color or other medium to a solid surface.

4. The art of paper folding.

7. The process of forming vessels and other objects with clay and other ceramic materials.

10. A method by which yarn is manipulated to create a textile or fabric.

11. A group of physical, mental, and spiritual practices or disciplines.

13. The process of assigning a code to something for the purposes of classification or identification.

14. The practice of growing and cultivating plants.

Down:

1. The art of carving, modeling, welding, or otherwise producing figurative or abstract works of art in three dimensions.

3. The act of creating written work, such as stories, novels, or poems.

5. The method of cooking food that uses prolonged dry heat.

6. The complex cognitive process of decoding symbols to derive meaning.

8. Moving the body in a way that goes with the rhythm and style of music that is being played.

9. An outdoor activity which consists of walking in natural environments.

12. A board game of strategic skill for two players, played on a checkered board.

Board Games

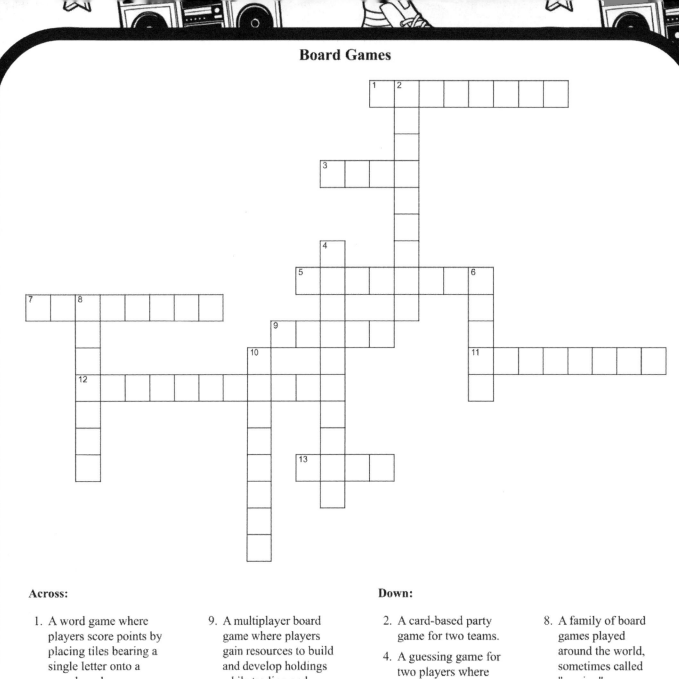

Across:

1. A word game where players score points by placing tiles bearing a single letter onto a gameboard.

3. A murder mystery game for three to six players.

5. A cooperative board game in which players work as a team to treat infections around the world while gathering resources for cures.

7. A deck-building card game.

9. A multiplayer board game where players gain resources to build and develop holdings while trading and acquiring resources.

11. A strategy board game for two players on a 10×10 square board.

12. A tile-based German-style board game.

13. A strategy board game of diplomacy, conflict and conquest.

Down:

2. A card-based party game for two teams.

4. A guessing game for two players where players try to guess the location of the other's ships.

6. A two-player strategy board game played on a checkered gameboard with 64 squares arranged in an 8×8 grid.

8. A family of board games played around the world, sometimes called "sowing" games.

10. A multi-player economics-themed board game.

Teenage Activists

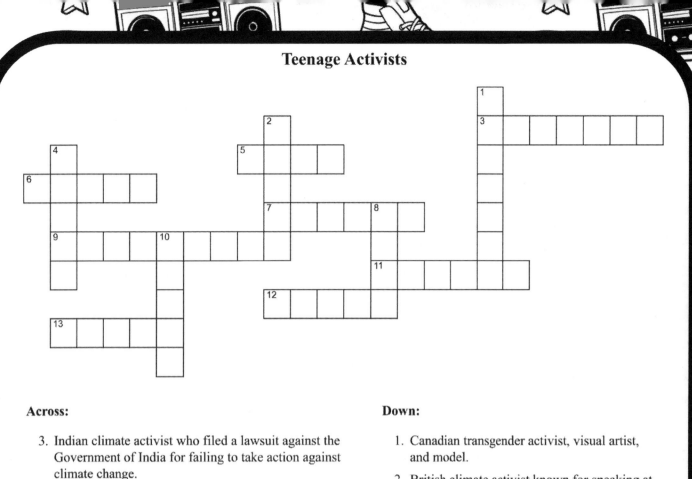

Across:

3. Indian climate activist who filed a lawsuit against the Government of India for failing to take action against climate change.

5. American YouTube personality, spokesmodel, television personality, and LGBTQ+ rights activist.

6. An American activist and advocate for gun control who is a survivor of the Stoneman Douglas High School shooting.

7. An American activist and feminist who launched a campaign called #1000BlackGirlBooks in November 2015.

9. Pakistani activist for female education and the youngest Nobel Prize laureate.

11. A Pakistani activist for female education and the youngest Nobel Prize laureate.

12. Swedish environmental activist on climate change whose campaigning has gained international recognition.

13. An American former actor, public speaker, and activist for food justice.

Down:

1. Canadian transgender activist, visual artist, and model.

2. British climate activist known for speaking at the 2019 Extinction Rebellion protests.

4. Indonesian environmental and climate activist.

8. American activist and advocate for gun control, who is a survivor of the Stoneman Douglas High School shooting.

10. American activist and advocate for the civil rights of Muslims.

FitnessTrends

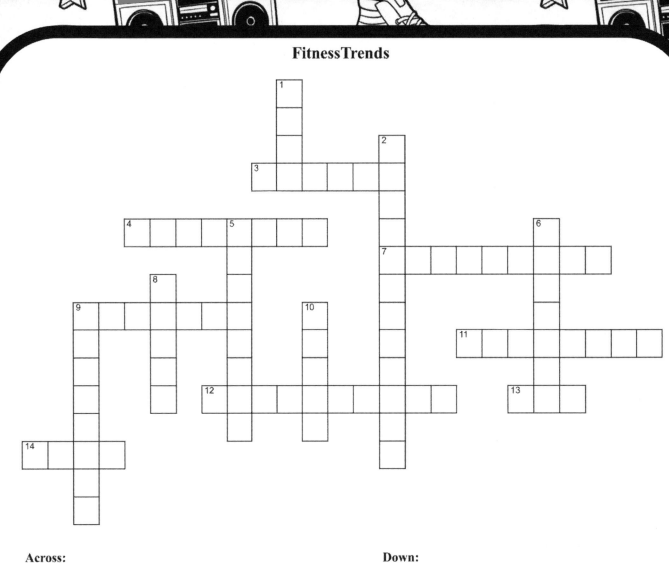

Across:

3. A high-intensity interval training workout, featuring exercises that last four minutes.

4. A type of group physical training program conducted by gyms, personal trainers, and former military personnel.

7. An indoor cycling class that provides an intense cardio workout.

9. A form of low-impact exercise that aims to strengthen muscles while improving postural alignment and flexibility.

11. A form of physical exercise that combines rhythmic aerobic exercise with stretching and strength training routines with the goal of improving all elements of fitness.

12. A group of stand-up combat sports based on kicking and punching, historically developed from karate mixed with boxing.

13. A form of suspension training that uses body weight exercises to develop strength, balance, flexibility and core stability simultaneously.

14. High Intensity Interval Training, a cardiovascular exercise strategy alternating short periods of intense anaerobic exercise with less intense recovery periods.

Down:

1. A mind and body practice with historical origins in ancient Indian philosophy.

2. A form of exercise consisting of a variety of movements which exercise large muscle groups.

5. A branded fitness regimen created by Greg Glassman.

6. A training discipline using movement that developed from military obstacle course training.

8. A form of physical exercise, usually conducted in group classes in gyms or specialty studios.

9. An activity that combines jogging with picking up litter.

10. A fitness program that combines Latin and international music with dance moves.

Coding Languages

Across:

3. A family of two high-level, general-purpose, interpreted, dynamic programming languages.

6. An interpreted, high-level, general-purpose programming language.

8. A programming language that conforms to the ECMAScript specification.

10. A cross-platform, statically typed, general-purpose programming language with type inference.

11. A multi-paradigm numerical computing environment and proprietary programming language developed by MathWorks.

12. A high-level general-purpose programming language.

Down:

1. A standard language for managing data held in a relational database management system.

2. A client-optimized programming language for apps on multiple platforms.

4. A high-level, general-purpose programming language designed for performance and safety, especially safe concurrency.

5. A powerful and intuitive programming language for macOS, iOS, watchOS, and tvOS.

7. A general-purpose, multi-paradigm programming language encompassing static typing, strong typing, lexically scoped, imperative, declarative, functional, generic, object-oriented (class-based), and component-oriented programming disciplines.

8. A class-based, object-oriented programming language that is designed to have as few implementation dependencies as possible.

9. A language and environment for statistical computing and graphics.

Social Media Platforms

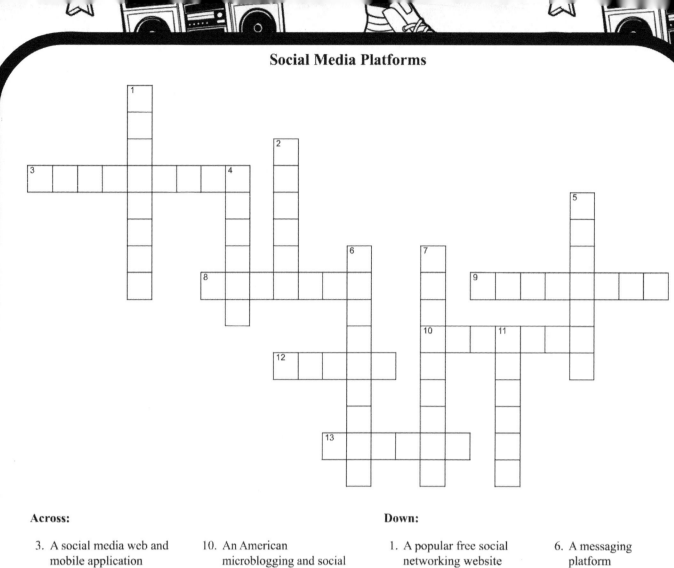

Across:

3. A social media web and mobile application company that operates a software system designed to discover information on the World Wide Web.

8. A video sharing service where users can watch, like, share, comment and upload their own videos.

9. A popular messaging app that lets users exchange pictures and videos that disappear after being viewed.

10. An American microblogging and social networking service on which users post and interact with messages known as "tweets".

12. A cross-platform voice over IP and instant messaging software application.

13. A Chinese multi-purpose messaging, social media and mobile payment app developed by Tencent.

Down:

1. A popular free social networking website that allows registered users to create profiles, upload photos and video.

2. A network of communities based on people's interests.

4. A social media app where users can post short-form videos.

5. A VoIP, instant messaging and digital distribution platform designed for creating communities.

6. A messaging platform developed by Facebook, originally Facebook Chat.

7. A photo and video sharing social networking service owned by Facebook, Inc.

11. A place to express yourself, discover yourself, and bond over the stuff you love.

Young Athletes

Across:

2. Japanese professional tennis player.

3. English professional footballer who plays as a winger, left-back or central midfielder for Premier League club Arsenal and the England national team.

6. Slovenian professional basketball player for the Dallas Mavericks of the National Basketball Association.

10. Japanese professional basketball player for the Washington Wizards of the National Basketball Association.

11. Dutch professional footballer who plays as a centre-back for Serie A club Juventus and the Netherlands national team.

12. Dominican professional baseball outfielder for the Washington Nationals of Major League Baseball.

13. Ukrainian professional tennis player.

15. American professional basketball player for the New Orleans Pelicans of the National Basketball Association.

Down:

1. American professional basketball player for the Memphis Grizzlies of the National Basketball Association.

4. American artistic gymnast with a combined total of 30 Olympic and World Championship medals.

5. American two-time Olympic gold medalist and World Cup alpine skier.

7. Dominican professional baseball shortstop for the San Diego Padres of Major League Baseball.

8. Norwegian professional footballer who plays as a striker for Borussia Dortmund and the Norway national team.

9. Spanish professional footballer who plays as a forward for Barcelona and the Spain national team.

14. French professional footballer who plays as a forward for Paris Saint-Germain and the France national team.

VideoGames

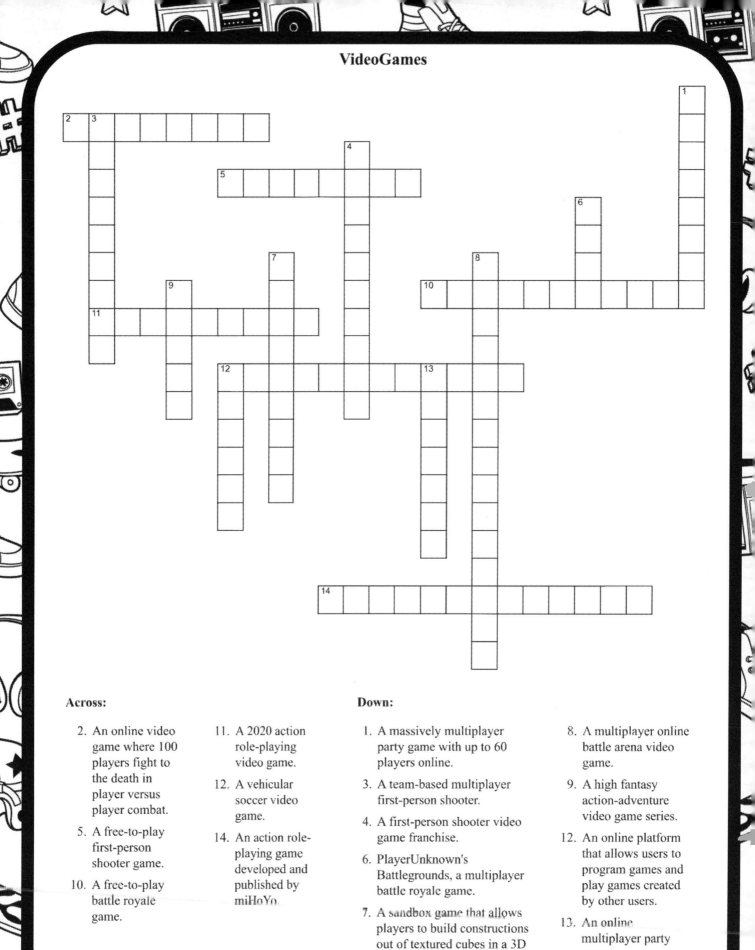

Across:

2. An online video game where 100 players fight to the death in player versus player combat.

5. A free-to-play first-person shooter game.

10. A free-to-play battle royale game.

11. A 2020 action role-playing video game.

12. A vehicular soccer video game.

14. An action role-playing game developed and published by miHoYo.

Down:

1. A massively multiplayer party game with up to 60 players online.

3. A team-based multiplayer first-person shooter.

4. A first-person shooter video game franchise.

6. PlayerUnknown's Battlegrounds, a multiplayer battle royale game.

7. A sandbox game that allows players to build constructions out of textured cubes in a 3D procedurally generated world.

8. A multiplayer online battle arena video game.

9. A high fantasy action-adventure video game series.

12. An online platform that allows users to program games and play games created by other users.

13. An online multiplayer party game.

Superheroes

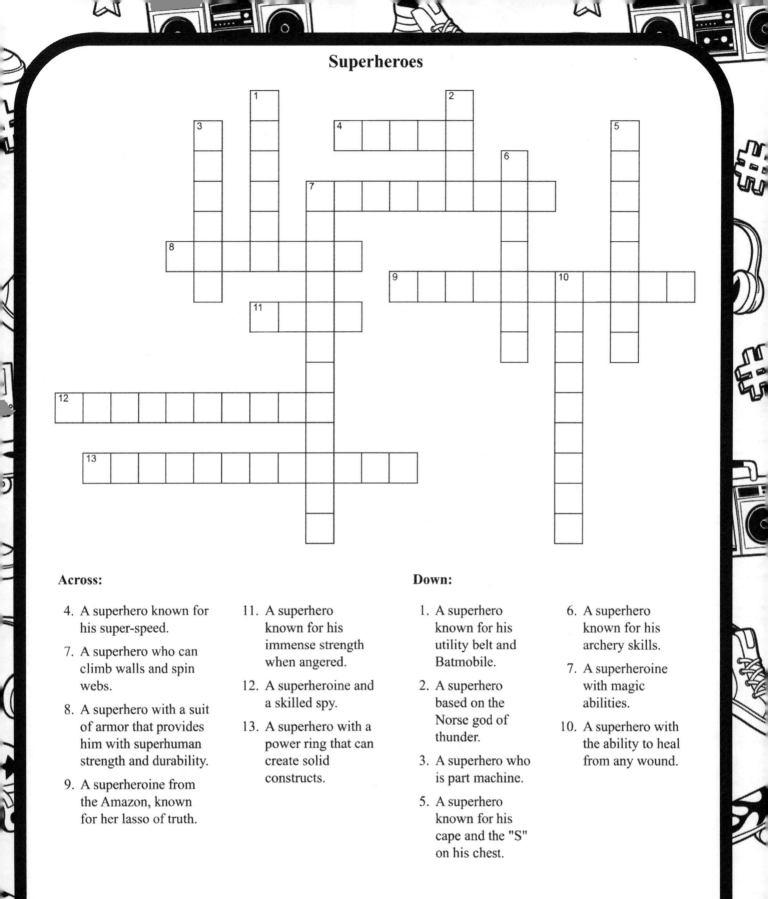

Across:

4. A superhero known for his super-speed.

7. A superhero who can climb walls and spin webs.

8. A superhero with a suit of armor that provides him with superhuman strength and durability.

9. A superheroine from the Amazon, known for her lasso of truth.

11. A superhero known for his immense strength when angered.

12. A superheroine and a skilled spy.

13. A superhero with a power ring that can create solid constructs.

Down:

1. A superhero known for his utility belt and Batmobile.

2. A superhero based on the Norse god of thunder.

3. A superhero who is part machine.

5. A superhero known for his cape and the "S" on his chest.

6. A superhero known for his archery skills.

7. A superheroine with magic abilities.

10. A superhero with the ability to heal from any wound.

Viral Challenges

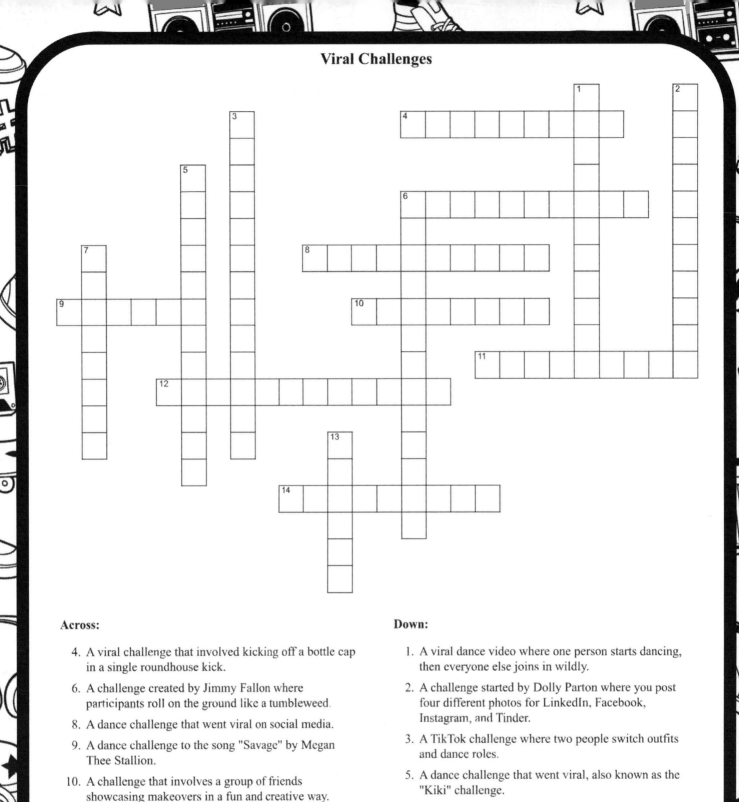

Across:

4. A viral challenge that involved kicking off a bottle cap in a single roundhouse kick.

6. A challenge created by Jimmy Fallon where participants roll on the ground like a tumbleweed.

8. A dance challenge that went viral on social media.

9. A dance challenge to the song "Savage" by Megan Thee Stallion.

10. A challenge that involves a group of friends showcasing makeovers in a fun and creative way.

11. A viral internet video trend where people remain frozen in action like mannequins while a moving camera films them.

12. Referring to the numerous dance trends that have emerged from the app.

14. A challenge to promote awareness of the disease amyotrophic lateral sclerosis (ALS) and encourage donations to research.

Down:

1. A viral dance video where one person starts dancing, then everyone else joins in wildly.

2. A challenge started by Dolly Parton where you post four different photos for LinkedIn, Facebook, Instagram, and Tinder.

3. A TikTok challenge where two people switch outfits and dance roles.

5. A dance challenge that went viral, also known as the "Kiki" challenge.

6. A challenge where three people hold each other's shoulders and jump between each other.

7. A challenge where you lie face down in an unusual or incongruous location.

13. A humorous social media event to storm Area 51, a U.S. Air Force facility.

Popular Apps

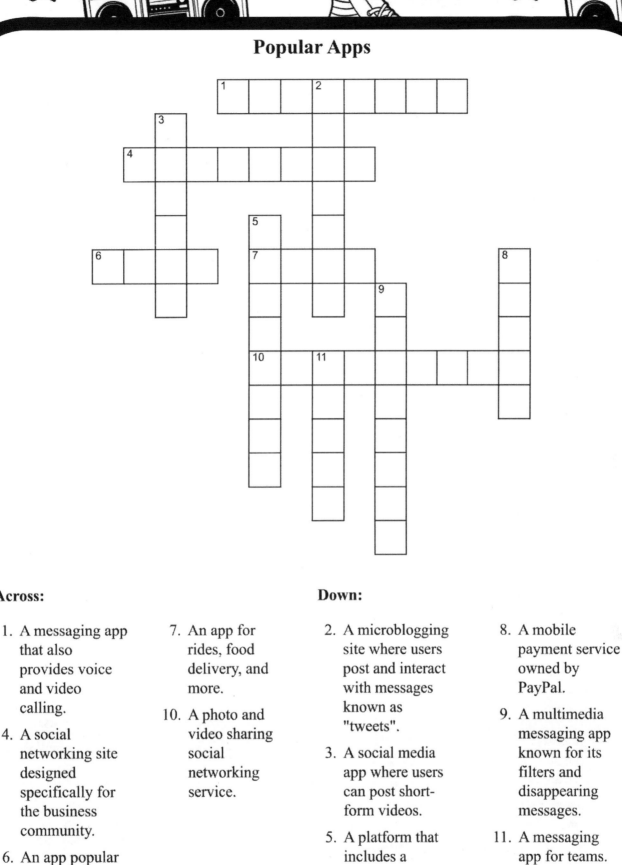

Across:

1. A messaging app that also provides voice and video calling.

4. A social networking site designed specifically for the business community.

6. An app popular for video conferencing.

7. An app for rides, food delivery, and more.

10. A photo and video sharing social networking service.

Down:

2. A microblogging site where users post and interact with messages known as "tweets".

3. A social media app where users can post short-form videos.

5. A platform that includes a language-learning website and app.

8. A mobile payment service owned by PayPal.

9. A multimedia messaging app known for its filters and disappearing messages.

11. A messaging app for teams.

Sports Stars

Across:

5. Spanish professional tennis player known as the "King of Clay".

7. Portuguese professional footballer often considered one of the best players in the world.

9. American professional football player, considered one of the greatest quarterbacks of all time.

10. British racing driver who competes in Formula One.

12. The most decorated Olympian of all time, a swimmer.

13. The last name of a famous tennis playing sister duo, Serena and Venus.

Down:

1. American professional basketball player known for his scoring ability.

2. Last name of a famous American football quarterback, Tom.

3. Japanese professional tennis player.

4. American professional basketball player known for his three-point shooting.

6. American professional basketball player often compared to Michael Jordan.

8. Jamaican retired sprinter, the fastest man in the world.

11. Argentine professional footballer who is considered one of the greatest players of all time.

Teenage Fashion Brands

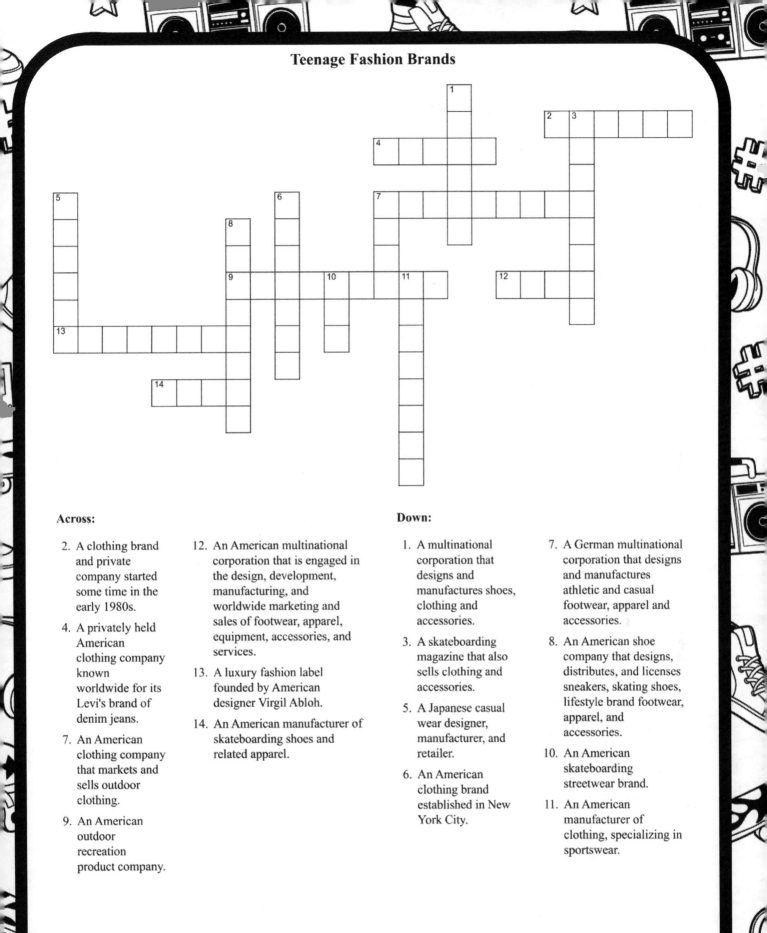

Across:

2. A clothing brand and private company started some time in the early 1980s.

4. A privately held American clothing company known worldwide for its Levi's brand of denim jeans.

7. An American clothing company that markets and sells outdoor clothing.

9. An American outdoor recreation product company.

12. An American multinational corporation that is engaged in the design, development, manufacturing, and worldwide marketing and sales of footwear, apparel, equipment, accessories, and services.

13. A luxury fashion label founded by American designer Virgil Abloh.

14. An American manufacturer of skateboarding shoes and related apparel.

Down:

1. A multinational corporation that designs and manufactures shoes, clothing and accessories.

3. A skateboarding magazine that also sells clothing and accessories.

5. A Japanese casual wear designer, manufacturer, and retailer.

6. An American clothing brand established in New York City.

7. A German multinational corporation that designs and manufactures athletic and casual footwear, apparel and accessories.

8. An American shoe company that designs, distributes, and licenses sneakers, skating shoes, lifestyle brand footwear, apparel, and accessories.

10. An American skateboarding streetwear brand.

11. An American manufacturer of clothing, specializing in sportswear.

Teen TV Shows

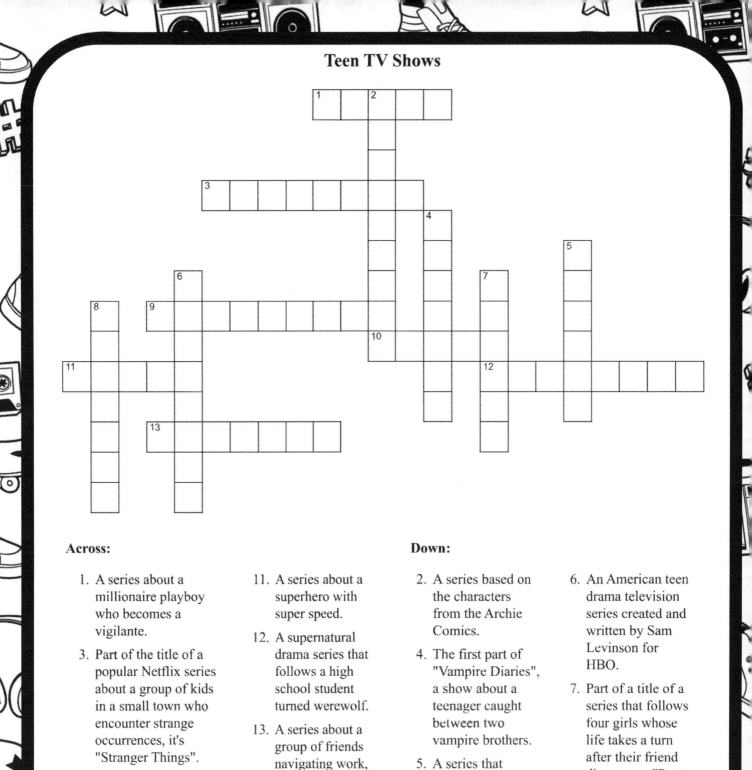

Across:

1. A series about a millionaire playboy who becomes a vigilante.

3. Part of the title of a popular Netflix series about a group of kids in a small town who encounter strange occurrences, it's "Stranger Things".

9. A series about Superman's cousin who also has superpowers.

10. A Spanish thriller teen drama series on Netflix.

11. A series about a superhero with super speed.

12. A supernatural drama series that follows a high school student turned werewolf.

13. A series about a group of friends navigating work, life, and love in New York City.

Down:

2. A series based on the characters from the Archie Comics.

4. The first part of "Vampire Diaries", a show about a teenager caught between two vampire brothers.

5. A series that follows a group of young superheroes.

6. An American teen drama television series created and written by Sam Levinson for HBO.

7. Part of a title of a series that follows four girls whose life takes a turn after their friend disappears, "Pretty Little Liars".

8. The second part of "Gilmore Girls", a show about a single mother and her daughter in a small town.

College Majors

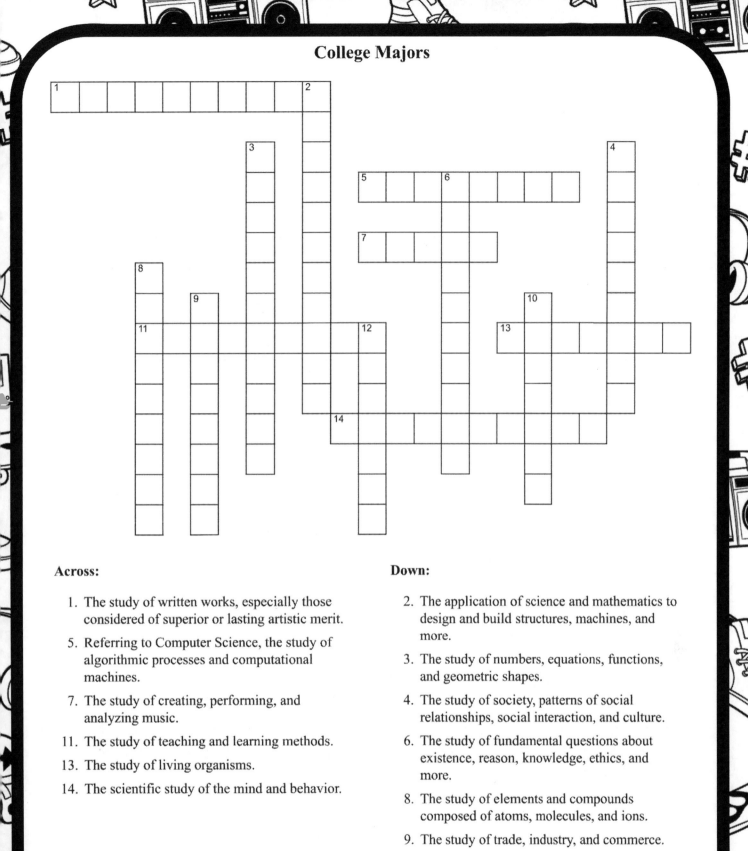

Across:

1. The study of written works, especially those considered of superior or lasting artistic merit.

5. Referring to Computer Science, the study of algorithmic processes and computational machines.

7. The study of creating, performing, and analyzing music.

11. The study of teaching and learning methods.

13. The study of living organisms.

14. The scientific study of the mind and behavior.

Down:

2. The application of science and mathematics to design and build structures, machines, and more.

3. The study of numbers, equations, functions, and geometric shapes.

4. The study of society, patterns of social relationships, social interaction, and culture.

6. The study of fundamental questions about existence, reason, knowledge, ethics, and more.

8. The study of elements and compounds composed of atoms, molecules, and ions.

9. The study of trade, industry, and commerce.

10. The study of past events.

12. A healthcare profession focused on the care of individuals and communities.

High School Subjects

Across:

1. The study of living organisms and their structures, life-cycles, adaptations, and environment.

3. The social science that studies the production, distribution, and consumption of goods and services.

6. The study of literature, composition, and grammar.

7. A branch of mathematics that uses letters and symbols to represent numbers in equations.

10. A Romance language of the Indo-European family.

11. The study of past events, particularly in human affairs.

12. The science of matter and energy and their interactions.

Down:

2. The study of places and the relationships between people and their environments.

4. The branch of science that deals with the identification of substances that matter is composed of.

5. A language that originated in the Castile region of Spain.

7. A subject where students learn to create visual or performing arts.

8. The subject that involves creating, performing, and analyzing music.

9. The study of acting, theater, and performance.

Anime Series

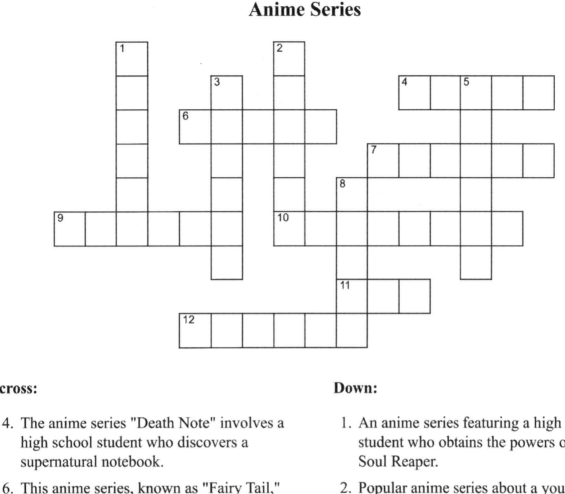

Across:

4. The anime series "Death Note" involves a high school student who discovers a supernatural notebook.

6. This anime series, known as "Fairy Tail," follows a celestial spirit mage, Lucy Heartfilia, after she joins the Fairy Tail Guild and teams up with Natsu Dragneel.

7. Known as "Hunter x Hunter," this anime is about a young boy who follows in his father's footsteps to become a hunter.

9. An anime series, also known as "My Hero Academia," set in a world where superpowers are the norm.

10. This anime series follows the journey of Monkey D. Luffy and his pirate crew in order to find the greatest treasure ever left by the legendary Pirate, Gol D Roger.

11. An anime series called "One Punch Man" about a superhero who can defeat any opponent with a single punch.

12. This popular anime, also known as "Dragon Ball," follows the adventures of Goku.

Down:

1. An anime series featuring a high school student who obtains the powers of a Soul Reaper.

2. Popular anime series about a young ninja seeking recognition and dreaming of becoming the Hokage.

3. "Sailor Moon" is a famous anime about a group of magical girls.

5. This anime, also known as "Attack on Titan," focuses on the fight against giant humanoid creatures.

8. This anime, also known as "Demon Slayer," follows a boy who becomes a demon slayer after his family is slaughtered and his sister is turned into a demon.

Famous YouTubers

Across:

2. Known as Markiplier, he is an American YouTuber recognized for his "Let's Play" videos.

5. A beauty YouTuber and makeup artist, known for her makeup tutorials and product reviews.

6. Swedish YouTuber known for his game commentaries and vlogs, his channel is PewDiePie.

8. Older of the Paul brothers who are known for their vlogs on YouTube.

9. He is the young star of the YouTube channel Ryan's World, formerly Ryan ToysReview.

11. She is an American actress and YouTube personality known for her comedy sketches, full name Liza Koshy.

Down:

1. British YouTuber known for his Minecraft gameplays, better known as DanTDM.

3. An Irish YouTuber known for his Let's Play series, his YouTube alias is Jacksepticeye.

4. This YouTuber is better known as MrBeast, famous for his large-scale challenges and donation videos.

7. Known for her humorous and satirical videos, her full name is Jenna Marbles.

9. He is a professional gamer who rose to fame on Twitch and YouTube, best known as Ninja.

10. Dancer, singer, and YouTube personality known for her bows, better known as JoJo Siwa.

MusicGenres

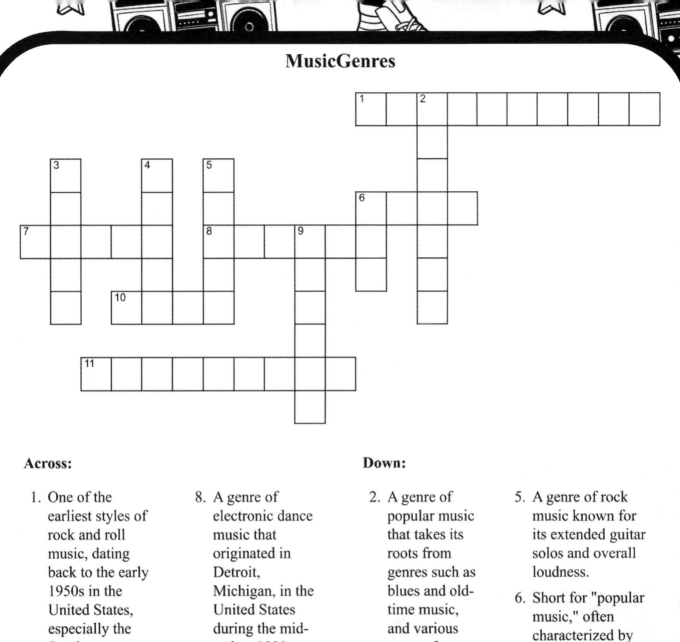

Across:

1. One of the earliest styles of rock and roll music, dating back to the early 1950s in the United States, especially the South.

6. Rock music genre that emerged in the mid-1970s characterized by fast, hard-edged music.

7. A music genre originated in the Deep South of the United States around the 1870s by African Americans.

8. A genre of electronic dance music that originated in Detroit, Michigan, in the United States during the mid-to-late 1980s.

10. Originated in the African American community in the United States in the 1950s and early 1960s.

11. A music style which originated in Puerto Rico during the late 1990s, characterized by Latin rhythms, dancehall, and hip-hop.

Down:

2. A genre of popular music that takes its roots from genres such as blues and old-time music, and various types of American folk music.

3. A popular form of social dance originating in Cuban folk dances.

4. A genre of dance music and a subculture that emerged in the 1970s from the United States' urban nightlife scene.

5. A genre of rock music known for its extended guitar solos and overall loudness.

6. Short for "popular music," often characterized by catchy melodies and lyrics.

9. A genre of popular music developed in the United States by inner-city African Americans and Latino Americans in the Bronx borough of New York City in the 1970s.

Young Adult Novels

Across:

2. Ally Condie's dystopian novel about a society where everything, including love, is decided by the government.

8. Rainbow Rowell's novel about two high school misfits who fall in love.

10. A dystopian novel by Lois Lowry about a society without pain or emotion.

11. John Green's novel about a boy attending boarding school and the enigmatic girl he befriends.

12. A novel by Jay Asher dealing with serious themes of suicide and its aftermath.

13. The first book of a dystopian trilogy by Suzanne Collins.

14. Marissa Meyer's retelling of Cinderella in a futuristic setting.

Down:

1. A series by Cassandra Clare about a secret society of demon hunters.

3. James Dashner's novel series about a group of boys trapped in a deadly maze.

4. A novel about a society divided into factions based on virtues.

5. A novel series about modern-day demigods by Rick Riordan.

6. Stephenie Meyer's novel series featuring a love triangle between a vampire, werewolf, and a human.

7. Kiera Cass's novel about a dystopian society where girls compete to be the future queen.

9. Scott Westerfeld's dystopian novel about a society obsessed with physical perfection.

SOLUTIONS

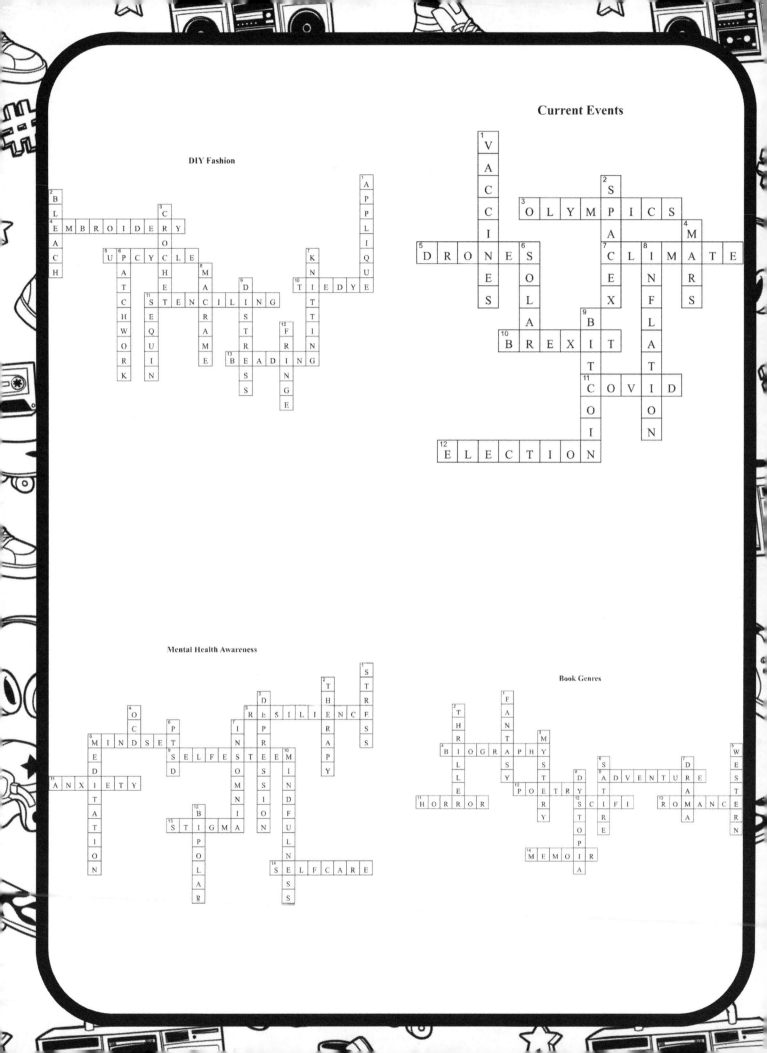

DIY Fashion

Current Events

Mental Health Awareness

Book Genres

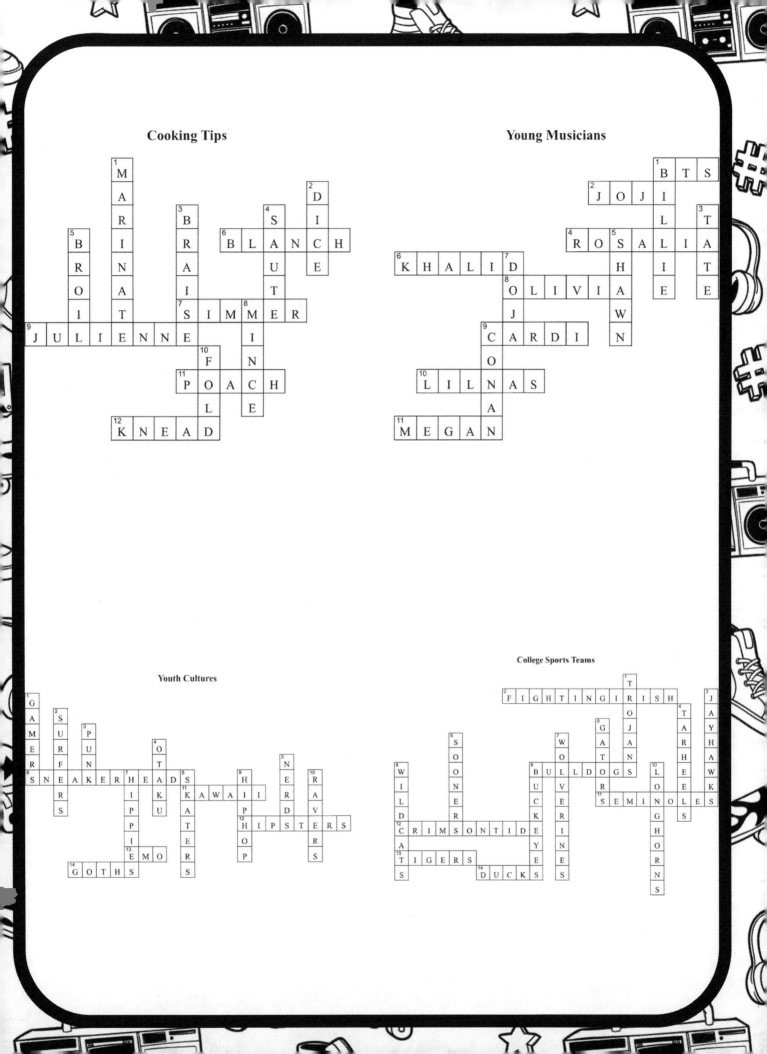

Popular Hashtags

Across:
1. LIKEFORLIKE
4. FOLLOWFORFOLLOW
5. LOVE
6. FOODPORN
9. THROWBACKTHURSDAY
11. OUTFITOFTHEDAY
12. SELFIE
13. INSTAMOOD
14. PHOTOOFTHEDAY
15. WANDERLUST

Down (letters):
2. INSTAGOOD
3. NOFILTER
7. NATUR
8. FITSPIRATION

Space Exploration

1. VENUS
2. SPACEX
3. JUNO
ROSCOSMOS
6. C
7. NASA
10. SPUTNIK
11. COMET
12. MARS
13. H O B B L E
14. GALILEO
9. K E P L E R
APOLLO

Dating Apps

1. MATCH
2. ZOOSK
3. OKCUPID
4. CLHNT
5. BUMBLE
6. TINDER
7. EHARMONY
8. HNE
9. HINGE
9. APPP
10. RAYA
11. GRINDR

Drawing Techniques

1. BLENDED
2. TONAL
3. ERASURE
5. DOODLING
6. STIPPLING
7. TRACING
8. PERSPECTIVE
9. GESTURAL
10. HATCHING
11. SCUMBLING
12. CONTOUR
13. CROSSHATCHING
14. SKETCHING

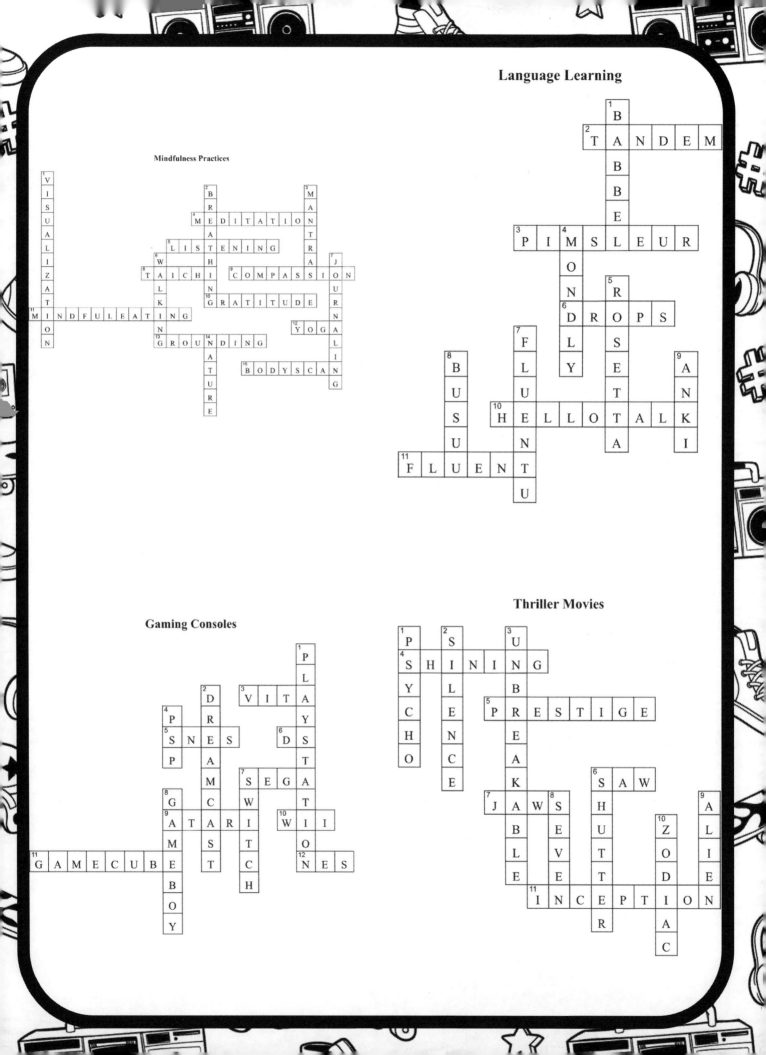

Language Learning

Mindfulness Practices

Gaming Consoles

Thriller Movies

Language Learning

Across:
2. TANDEM
3. PIMSLEUR
6. DROPS
10. HELLOTALK
11. FLUENT

Down:
1. BABBEL
4. MONDLY
5. ROSETTA
7. FLUENTU
8. BUSUU
9. ANKI

Mindfulness Practices

4. MEDITATION
5. LISTENING
8. TAICHI
9. COMPASSION
10. GRATITUDE
11. MINDFULEATING
12. YOGA
13. GROUNDING
15. BODYSCAN

Down:
1. VISUALIZATION
2. BRAIN
3. MANTRA
6. WALKING
7. JOURNALING
14. NATURE

Gaming Consoles

1. PLAYSTATION
2. DREAMCAST
3. VITA
4. PSP
5. SNES
6. DS
7. SWITCH
8. GAMEBOY
9. ATARI
10. WII
11. GAMECUBE
12. NES

Thriller Movies

1. PSYCHO
2. SILENCE
3. USUBEAK
4. SHINING
5. PRESTIGE
6. SAW
7. JAWS
8. SEVEN
9. ALIEN
10. ZODIAC
11. INCEPTION

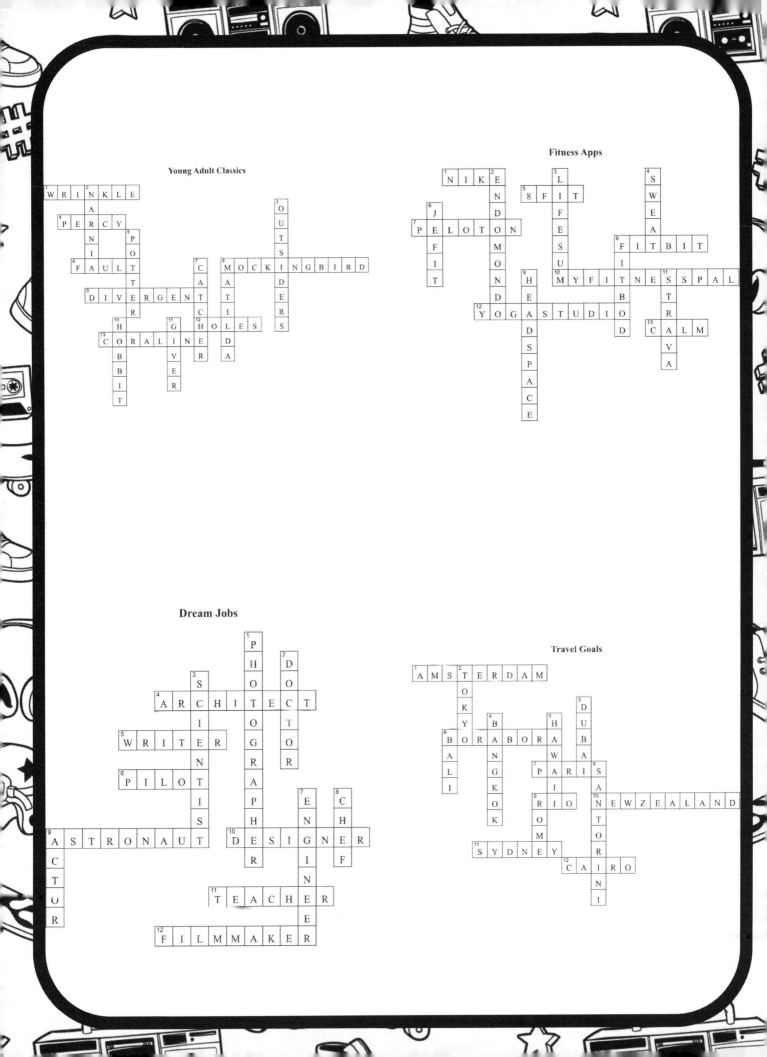

Young Adult Classics

WRINKLE · PERCY · FAULT · MOCKINGBIRD · DIVERGENT · CORALINE · HOLES · OUTSIDERS · CATCHER · POTTER · ANNIE · HOBBIT · GIVER · MATILDA

Fitness Apps

NIKE · 8FIT · PELOTON · FITBIT · MYFITNESSPAL · YOGASTUDIO · CALM · LIFESUM · ENDOMONDO · JFIT · SWEAT · HEADSPACE · BODY · STRAVA

Dream Jobs

ARCHITECT · WRITER · PILOT · ASTRONAUT · DESIGNER · TEACHER · FILMMAKER · PHOTOGRAPHER · DOCTOR · SCIENTIST · ENGINEER · CHEF · ACTOR

Travel Goals

AMSTERDAM · BORABORA · PARIS · NEWZEALAND · SYDNEY · CAIRO · TOKYO · DOHA · DUBAI · BANGKOK · HAWAII · BALI · RIO · ROME · SANTORINI

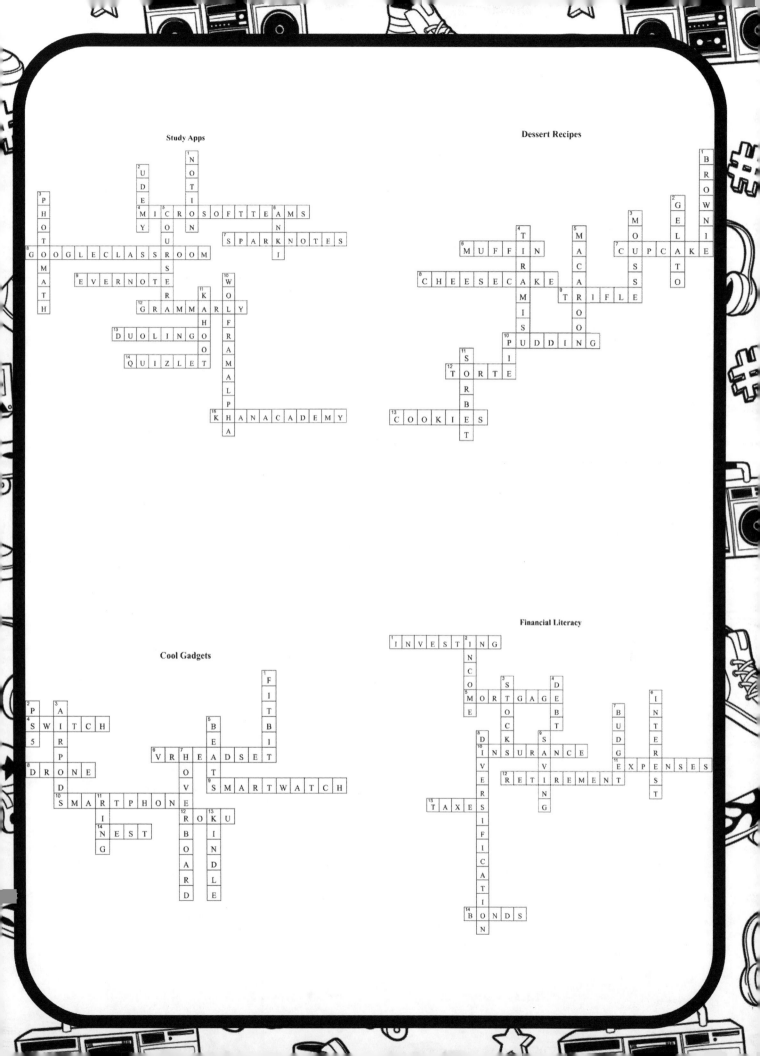

Study Apps

NOTION
UDEMY
PHOTOMATH
MICROSOFTTEAMS
YOURSE
SPARKNOTES
GOOGLECLASSROOM
EVERNOTE
GRAMMARLY
KHANACADEMY
DUOLINGO
QUIZLET
WORDFRAMALPA

Dessert Recipes

BROWNI
GELATO
MOUSSE
TRAMISU
MUFFIN
MACAROON
CUPCAKE
CHEESECAKE
TRIFLE
PUDDING
SORBET
TORTE
COOKIES

Cool Gadgets

FITBIT
PARP
APPD
SWITCH
BEETSOVE
VRHEADSET
DRONE
SMARTWATCH
SMARTPHONE
ROKU
RING
NEST
BOARD
KINDLE

Financial Literacy

INVESTING
INCOME
MORTGAGE
STOCK
DEBT
SAVING
DIVERSIFICATION
BUDGET
INTEREST
INSURANCE
EXPENSES
RETIREMENT
TAXES
BONDS

Body Positivity

RADIANCE · INCLUSIVITY · ACCEPTANCE · NOURISHMENT · WELLBEING · JOY · INDIVIDUALITY · BALANCE · EMPOWERMENT · DIVERSITY · RESPECT · HEALTH · MOVEMENT · CONFIDENCE

Career Options

GOVERNMENT · MEDICINE · TECH · ART · LAW · SPORTS · ENGINEERING · FINANCE · SOCIALWORK · EDUCATION · COMMUNICATION · WRITING · ENTREPRENEURSHIP · SCIENCE

College Preparation

ESSAYWRITING · RECOMMENDATIONS · RESEARCH · FINANCIALAID · SUPPLIES · APPLICATION · EXTRACURRICULARS · SCHOLARSHIPS · MAJORCHOICE · HEALTH · VISITS · STANDARDIZEDTEST · HOUSING · INTERVIEW · DEADLINE

DIY Projects

ORIGAMI · MACRAME · JEWELRYMAKING · SEWING · TERRARIUMS · POTTERY · GARDENING · QUILTING · KNITTING · SCRAPBOOKING · WOODWORKING · CANDLEMAKING · EMBROIDERY · SOAPMAKING · PAINTING · HOMEBREWING

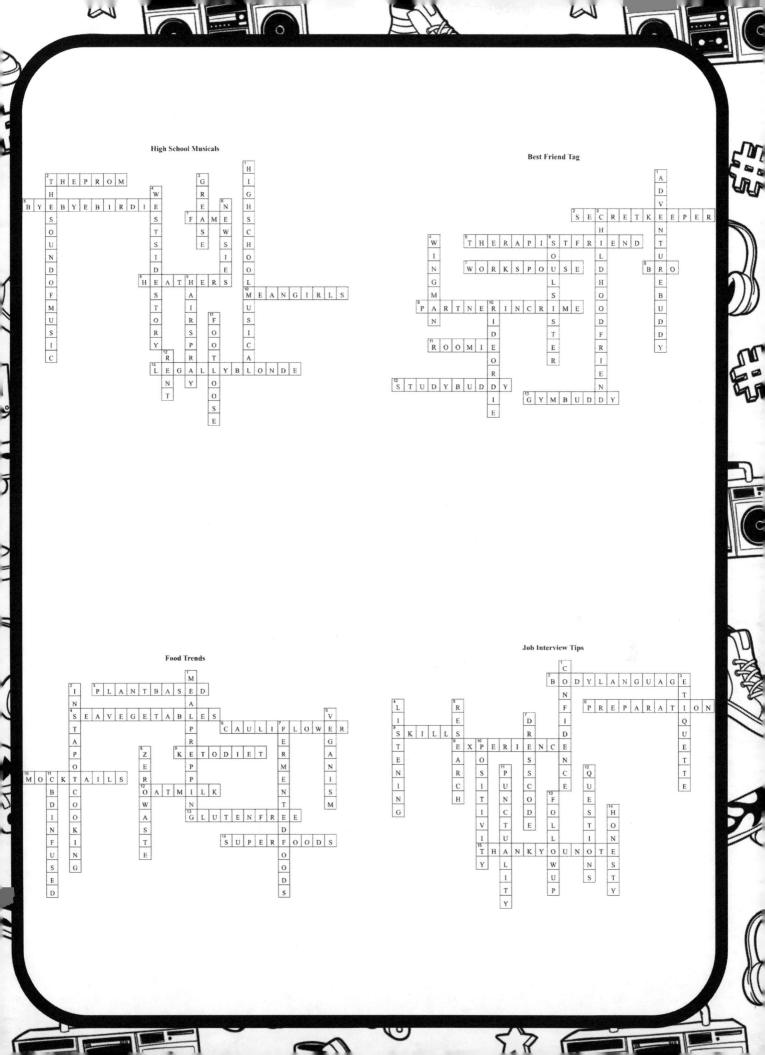

High School Musicals

Best Friend Tag

Food Trends

Job Interview Tips

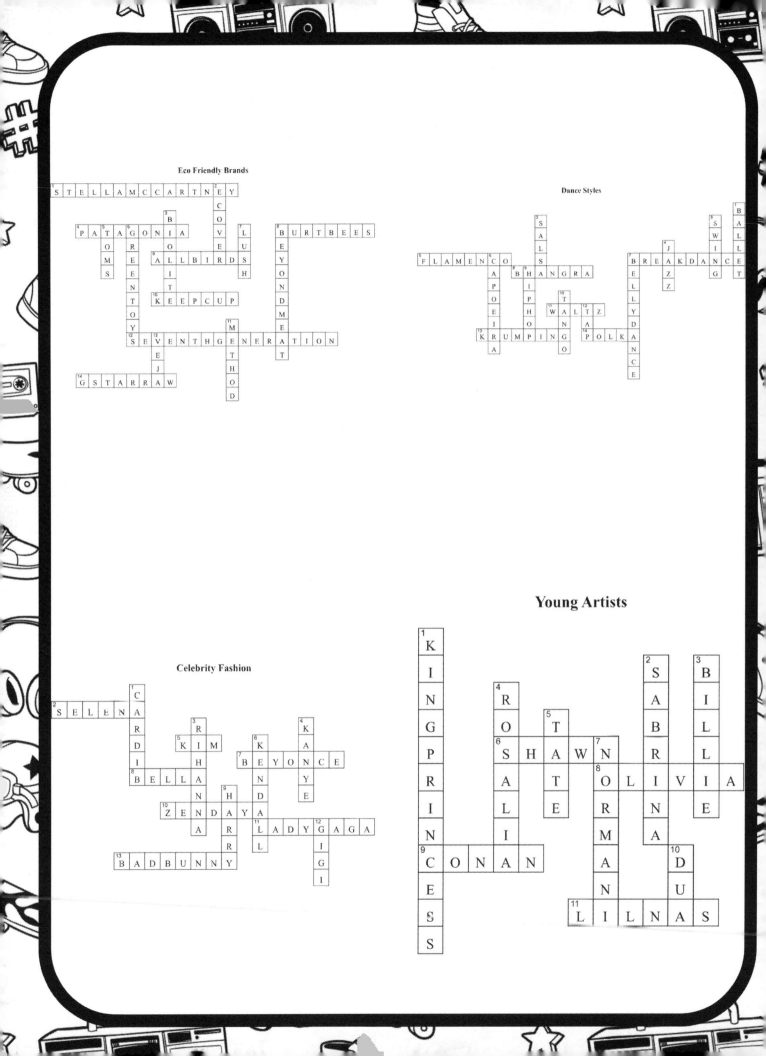

Eco Friendly Brands

STELLAMCCARTNEY
PATAGONIA
ALLBIRDS
KEEPCUP
SEVENTHGENERATION
GSTARRAW
BURTBEES

Dance Styles

FLAMENCO
BHANGRA
BREAKDANCE
WALTZ
KRUMPING
POLKA

Celebrity Fashion

SELENA
KIM
BEYONCE
BELLA
ZENDAYA
LADYGAGA
BADBUNNY

Young Artists

KINGPRINCESS
SHAWN
OLIVIA
CONAN
LILNAS

Streaming Services

- 2. TWITCH
- 4. ROKU
- 5. DISNEYPLUS
- 7. NETFLIX
- 9. APPLETV
- 11. HBOMAX

Down answers visible: CRUNCHYROLL, YOUTUBETV, HULU, APPLETVPRIME

Youth Sports

- 1. TRACK
- 2. WRESTLING
- 5. TENNIS
- 7. KARATE
- 9. SWIMMING
- 11. SOCCER
- 12. FOOTBALL
- 13. BASEBALL

Down: SKATEBOARDING, GYMNASTICS, FIELDHOCKEY, VOLLEYBALL, BASKETBALL, SURFING

Book Series

- 2. CHRONICLES
- 4. THRONE
- 9. INSTRUMENTS
- 11. DIVERGENT
- 13. MORTAL
- 14. HOBBIT
- 15. SNICKET

Down: GIVER, UNFORTUNATE, OLYMPIANS, HUNGER, PERCY, TWILIGHT, GAMES, POTTER

Social Justice Terms

- 2. DIVERSITY
- 5. PRIVILEGE
- 9. ABLEISM
- 11. XENOPHOBIA
- 12. ACTIVISM
- 13. INCLUSION
- 14. ALLYSHIP

Down: INTERSECTIONALITY, OPPRESSION, DISCRIMINATION, RACISM, FEMINISM, SEXISM, EQUALITY

Mobile Games

2 ROBLOX
4 AMONGUS
6 POKEMONGO
7 FRUITNINJA
8 FORTNITE
9 HELIXJUMP
11 SUBWAYSURFERS
12 MINECRAFT
13 TEMPLERUN
14 CROSSYROAD

Down clues (letters in grid):
- CAR HR YALE (CAR...)
- CALLOFDUTY
- ANGRYBIRDS
- CANDYCRUSH

Young Adult Authors

1 ANDERSON
4 CLARE
5 ROTH
7 ALBERTALLI
9 DASHNER
13 COLLINS
14 NIVEN

Down: RIORDAN, ADDIEH, GREEN, HAN, ROWLING, YOON, SNICKET

Study Abroad Destinations

1 MEXICO
4 FRANCE
5 ITALY
9 SWEDEN
10 CANADA
11 SPAIN
12 JAPAN

Down: CHINA, BRAZIL, AUSTRIA, IRELAND, GERMANY

Extracurricular Activities

2 DRAMA
5 NEWSPAPER
6 BAND
8 MATHLETE
9 ART
11 SCIENCECLUB
13 ECOCLUB
14 VOLUNTEER
15 ORCHESTRA

Down: CHOIR, ROBOTICS, DEBATE, YEARBOOK, FOOTBALL

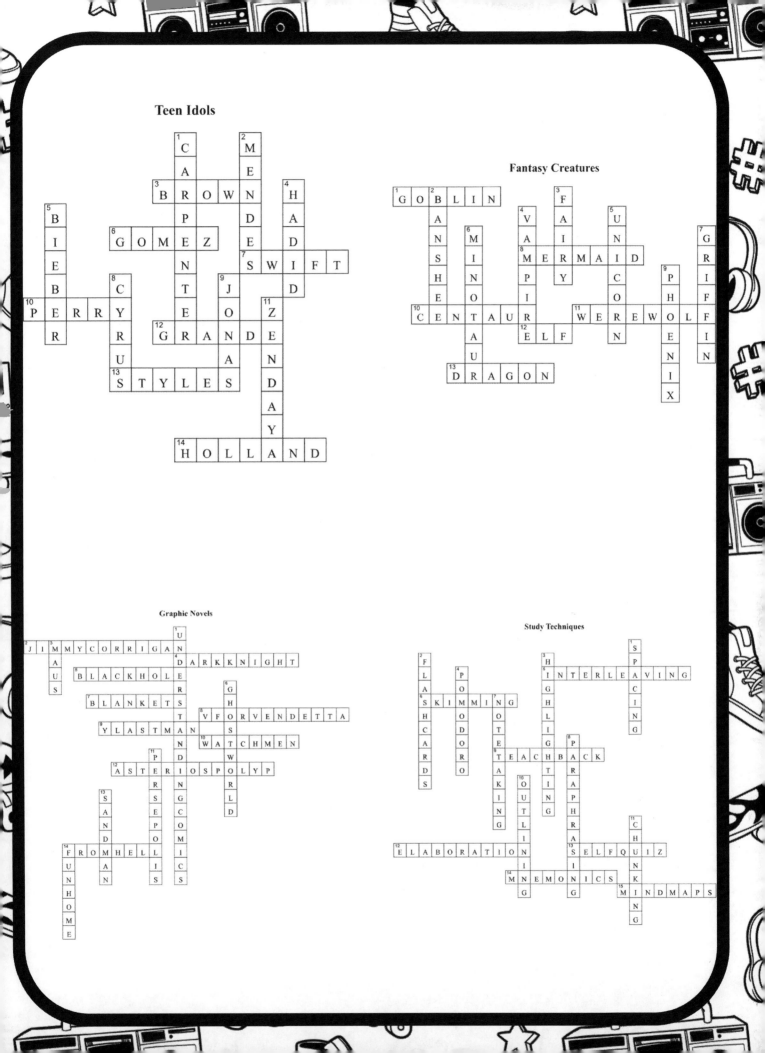

Teen Idols

Fantasy Creatures

Graphic Novels

Study Techniques

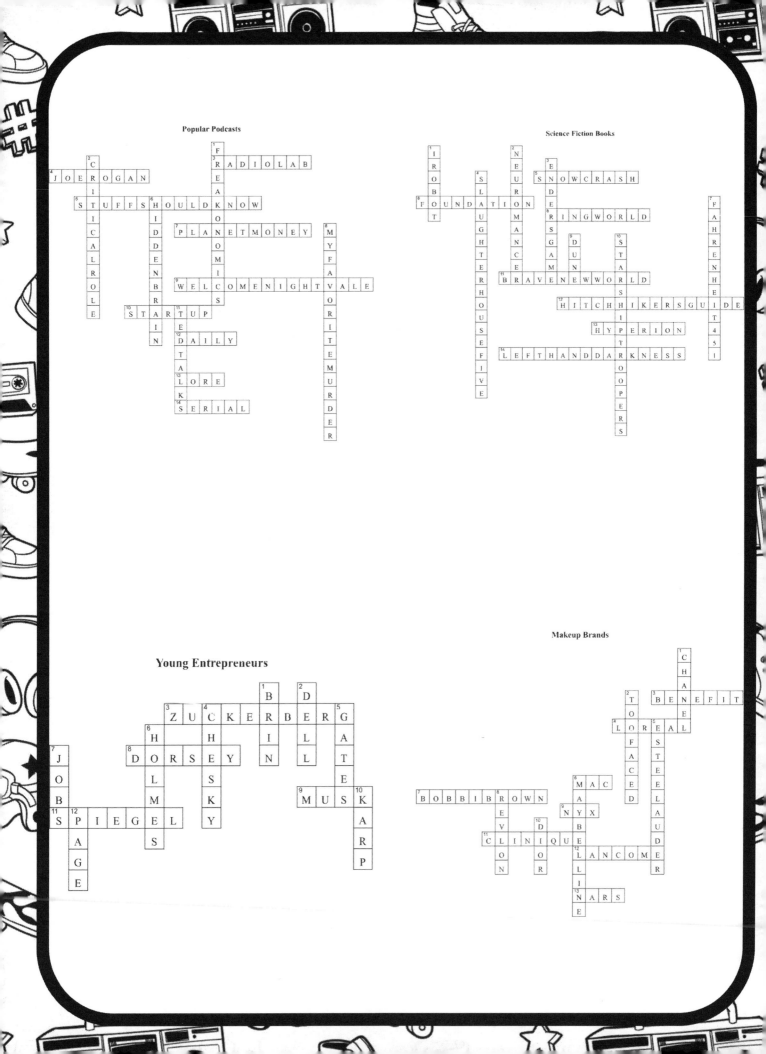

Popular Podcasts

Science Fiction Books

Young Entrepreneurs

Makeup Brands

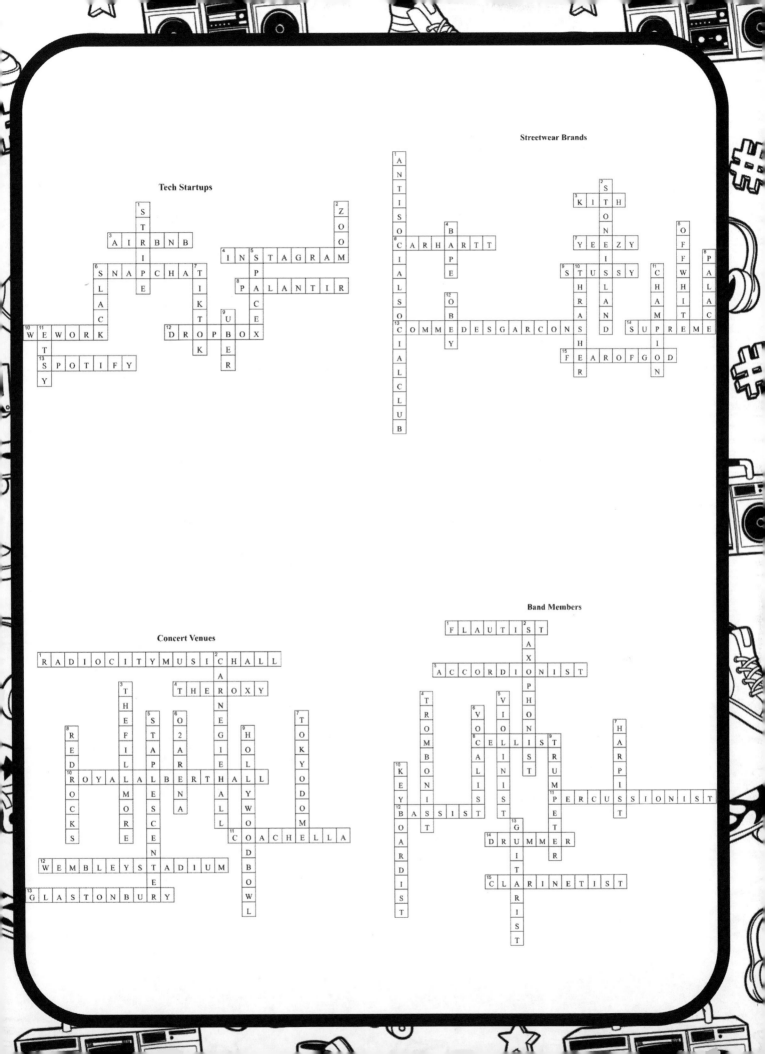

Tech Startups

Streetwear Brands

Concert Venues

Band Members

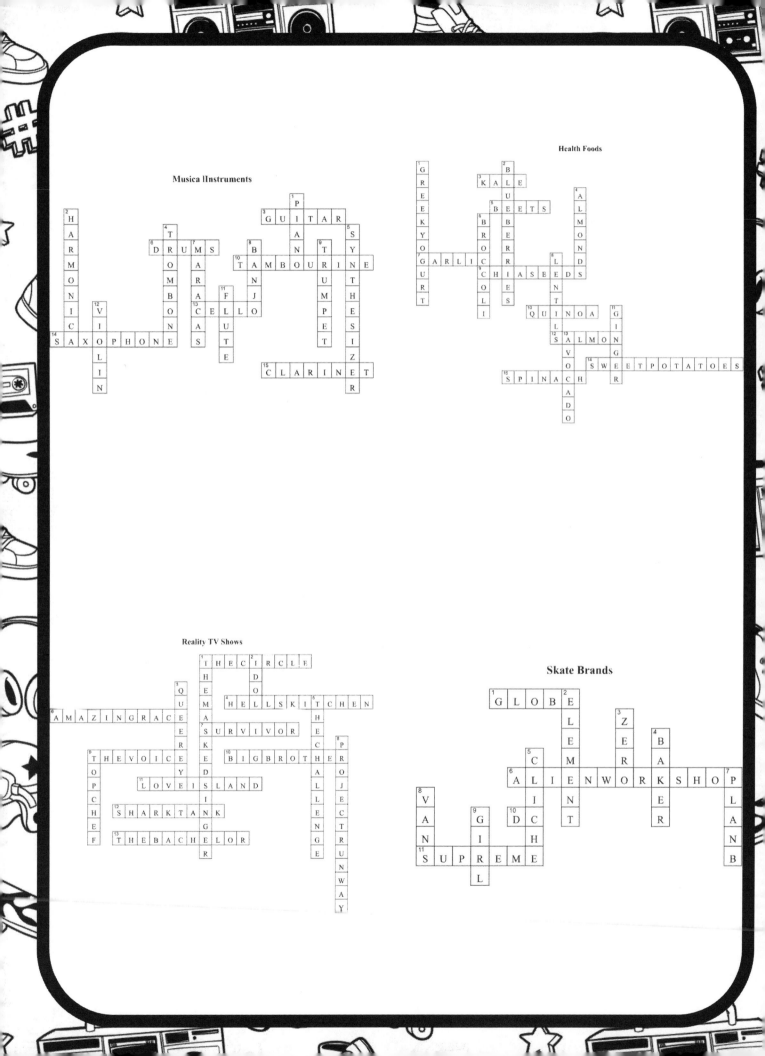

Musica lInstruments

P
GUITAR
H
T
DRUMS
B
TAMBOURINE
V
CELLO
SAXOPHONE
CLARINET

Health Foods

KALE
BEETS
GARLIC
CHIASEEDS
QUINOA
SALMON
SWEETPOTATOES
SPINACH

Reality TV Shows

THECIRCLE
HELLSKITCHEN
AMAZINGRACE
SURVIVOR
THEVOICE
BIGBROTHER
LOVEISLAND
SHARKTANK
THEBACHELOR

Skate Brands

GLOBE
ALIENWORKSHOP
VAN
SUPREME

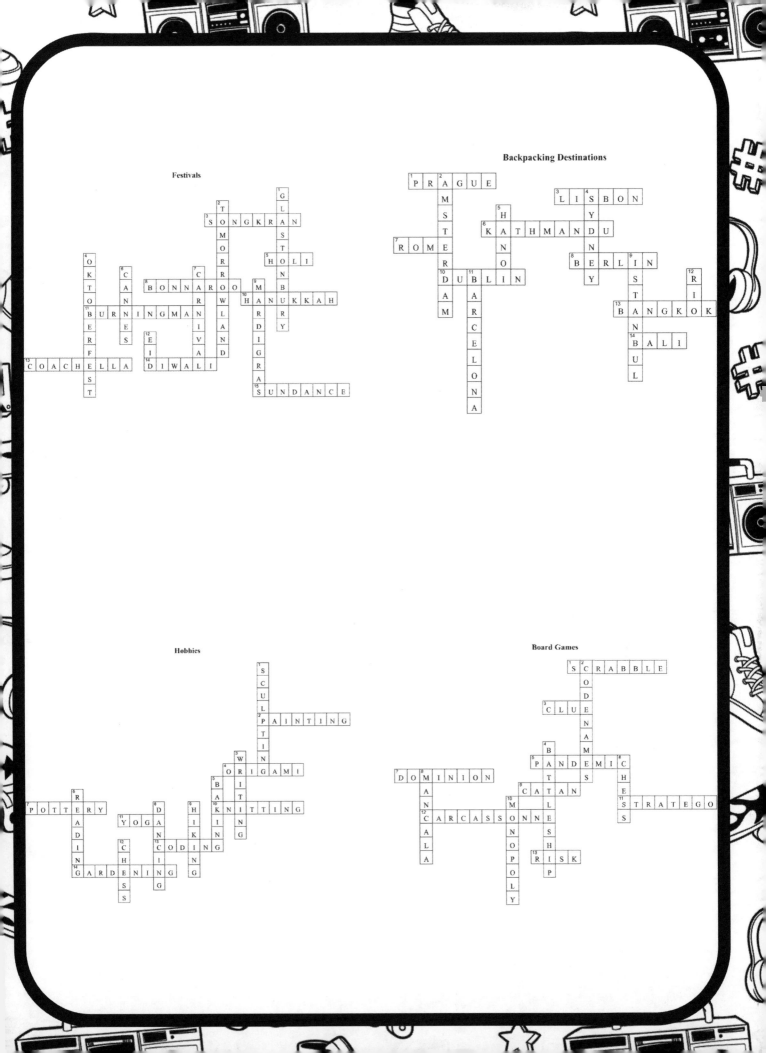

Festivals

Across
3. SONGKRAN
5. HOLI
8. BONNAROO
10. HANUKKAH
11. BURNINGMAN
13. COACHELLA
14. DIWALI
15. SUNDANCE

Down
1. GLASTONBURY
2. TOMORROWLAND
4. OKTOBERFEST
6. CANNES
7. CARNIVAL
9. MARDIGRAS
12. EID

Backpacking Destinations

Across
1. PRAGUE
3. LISBON
6. KATHMANDU
7. ROME
8. BERLIN
10. DUBLIN
13. BANGKOK
14. BALI

Down
2. AMSTERDAM
4. SYDNEY
5. HANOI
9. ISTANBUL
11. BARCELONA
12. RIO

Hobbies

Across
2. PAINTING
4. ORIGAMI
7. POTTERY
10. KNITTING
11. YOGA
13. CODING
14. GARDENING

Down
1. SCULPTING
3. WRITING
5. BAKING
6. READING
8. DANCING
9. HIKING
12. CHESS

Board Games

Across
1. SCRABBLE
3. CLUE
5. PANDEMIC
7. DOMINION
9. CATAN
11. STRATEGO
12. CARCASSONNE
13. RISK

Down
2. CODENAMES
4. BATTLESHIP
6. CHESS
8. AGRICOLA
10. MONOPOLY

Teenage Activists

Across / Down entries shown in grid:

- RIDHIMA
- JAMIE
- JAZZ
- MARLEY
- YOUSAFZAI
- MALALA
- GRETA
- HAILE

Down letters: BRISTOO, NOO, NDAAHMED, etc.

Grid letters:
- ¹B
- ²N
- ³R I D H I M A
- ⁴N
- ⁵J A Z Z
- ⁶J A M I E
- M A R L E Y
- ⁹Y O U S A F Z A I
- ¹¹M A L A L A
- ¹²G R E T A
- ¹³H A I L E

FitnessTrends

Grid letters:
- Y O G (YOGA)
- ²C
- ³T A B A T A
- ⁴B O O T C A M P
- ⁵C R O S S F I T
- SPINCLASS
- ⁶P
- ⁹P I L A T E S
- ⁸B A R R E
- ¹⁰Z U M B A
- ¹¹A E R O B I C S
- JOGGING
- ¹²K I C K B O X I N G
- ¹³T R X
- ¹⁴H I I T
- CALISTHENICS

Coding Languages

Grid letters:
- ¹S Q L
- ²D A R T
- ³P E R L
- ⁴L U A
- ⁵S W I F T
- ⁶R U B Y
- ⁷C S H A R P
- ⁸J A V A S C R I P T
- ⁹S C R I P T
- ¹⁰K O T L I N
- ¹¹M A T L A B
- ¹²P Y T H O N

Social Media Platforms

Grid letters:
- ¹F A C E B O O K
- ²R E D D I T
- ³P I N T E R E S T
- ⁴T I K T O K
- ⁵D I S C O R D
- ⁶M E S S E N G E R
- ⁷I N S T A G R A M
- ⁸Y O U T U B E
- ⁹S N A P C H A T
- ¹⁰T W I T T E R
- ¹¹T U M B L R
- ¹²V I B E R
- ¹³W E C H A T

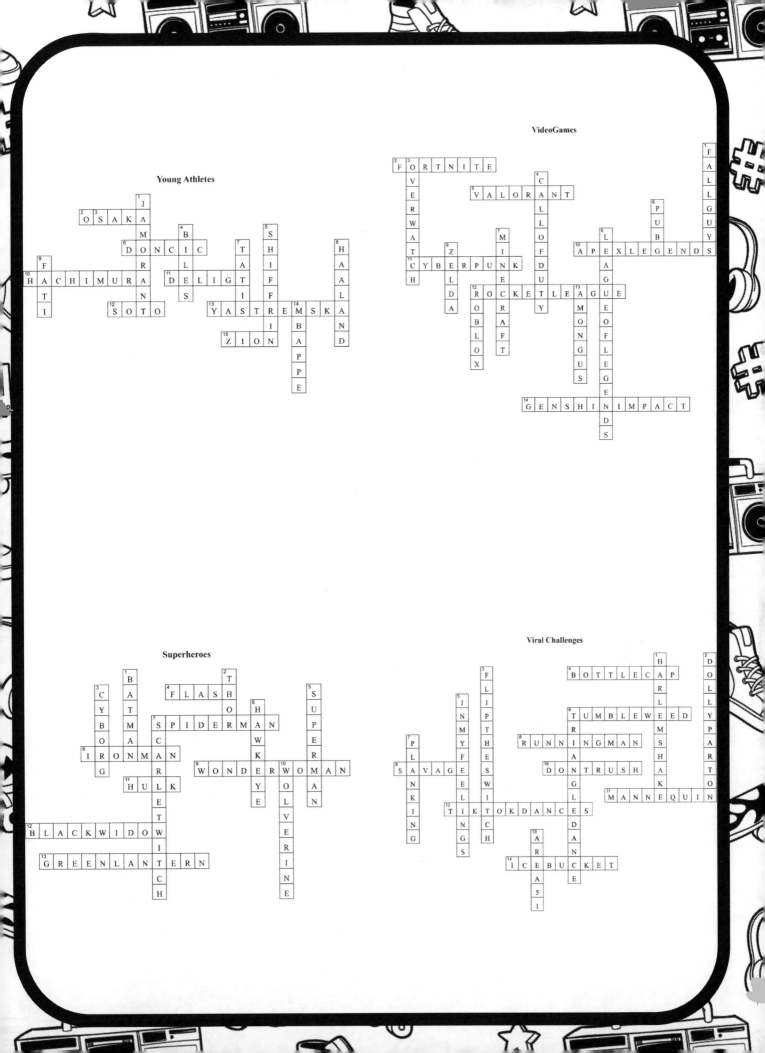

Young Athletes

VideoGames

Superheroes

Viral Challenges

Popular Apps

WHATSAPP
LINKEDIN
TIKTOK
ZOOM
UBER
DUOLINGO
INSTAGRAM
SLACK
SNAPCHAT
VENMO
TWITTER

Sports Stars

HARDEN
BRADY
OSAKA
CURRY
NADAL
RONALDO
BOLT
BRADY
HAMILTON
MESSI
PHELPS
WILLIAMS

Teenage Fashion Brands

ADIDAS
STUSSY
LEVIS
PATAGONIA
SUPREME
CARHARTT
SUPREME
NORTHFACE
HUF
CHAMPION
NIKE
UNIQLO
OFFWHITE
VANS

Teen TV Shows

ARROW
RIVERDALE
STRANGER
VAMPIRE
SUPERGIRL
PRETTY
GILMORE
ELITE
FLASH
TEENWOLF
EUPHORIA
FRIENDS
TITANS

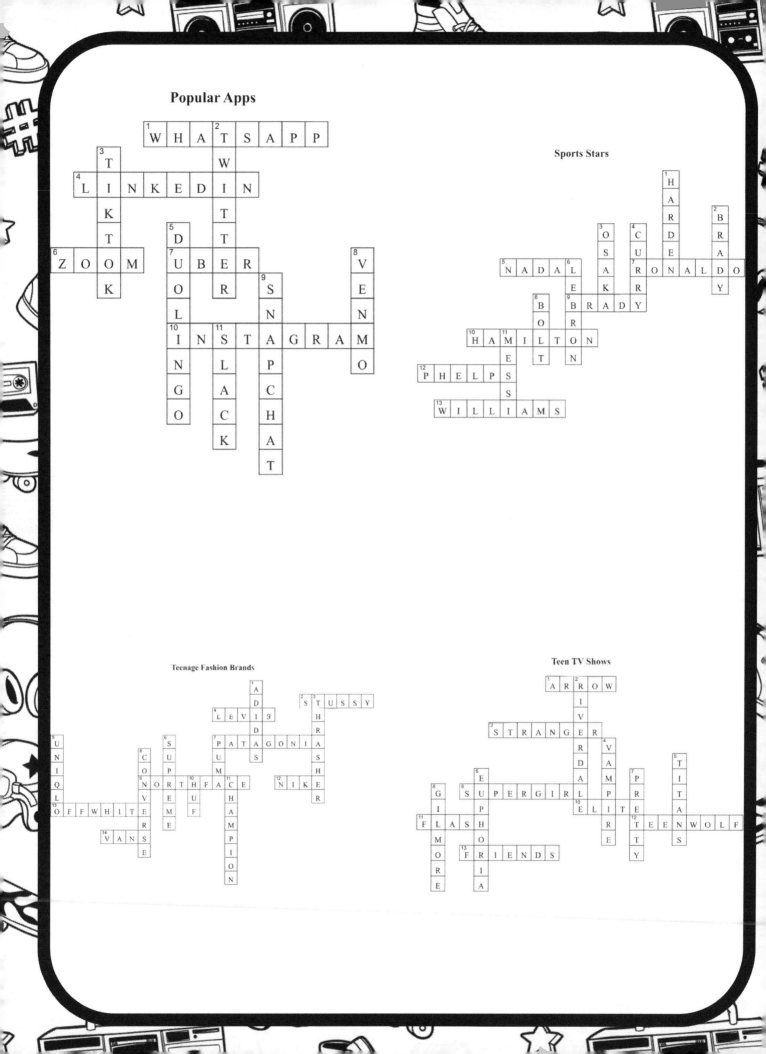

College Majors

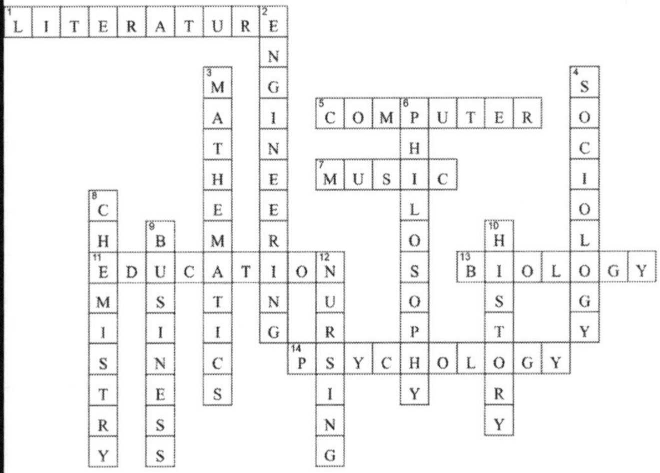

1 LITERATURE
2 ENGINEERING
3 MATHEMATICS
4 SOCIOLOGY
5 COMPUTER
6 PHILOSOPHY
7 MUSIC
8 CHEMISTRY
9 BUSINESS
10 HISTORY
11 EDUCATION
12 NURSING
13 BIOLOGY
14 PSYCHOLOGY

High School Subjects

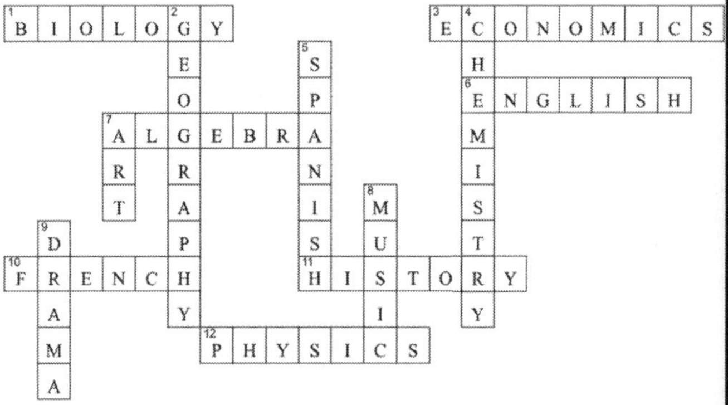

1 BIOLOGY
2 GEOGRAPHY
3 ECONOMICS
4 CHEMISTRY
5 SPANISH
6 ENGLISH
7 ALGEBRA
7 ART
8 MUSIC
9 DRAMA
10 FRENCH
11 HISTORY
12 PHYSICS

Anime Series

1 BLEACH
2 NARUTO
3 SAILOR
4 DEATH
5 ATTACK
6 FAIRY
7 HUNTER
8 DEMON
9 MYHERO
10 ONEPIECE
11 ONE
12 DRAGON

FamousYouTubers

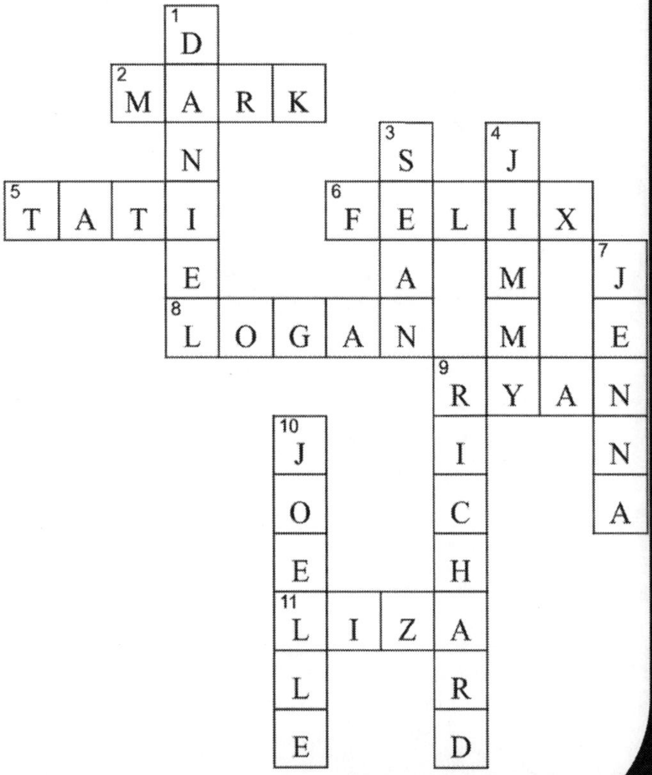

1 DANIEL
2 MARK
3 SEAN
4 JIMMY
5 TATI
6 FELIX
7 JENNA
8 LOGAN
9 RYAN
9 RICHARD
10 JOELLE
11 LIZA

MusicGenres

Music Genres crossword:

- 1 across: ROCKABILLY
- 2 down: COUNTRY
- 3 down: SASSA
- 4 down: DIE
- 5 down: ME
- 6 down/across: PUNK
- 7 across: BLUES
- 8 across: TECHNO
- 9 down: HIPHOP
- 10 across: SOUL
- 11 across: REGGAETON

Young Adult Novels crossword:

- 1 down: SHADOWHUNTER
- 2 across: MATCHED
- 3 down: MAZS (MAZE)
- 4 down: DIVERGE(N)T
- 5 down: PERCY
- 6 down: TWILIGHT
- 7 down: SULLC
- 8 across: ELEANOR
- 9 across: GIVER
- 10 across: GIVER
- 11 across: LOOKING
- 12 across: THIRTEEN
- 13 across: HUNGER
- 14 across: CINDER

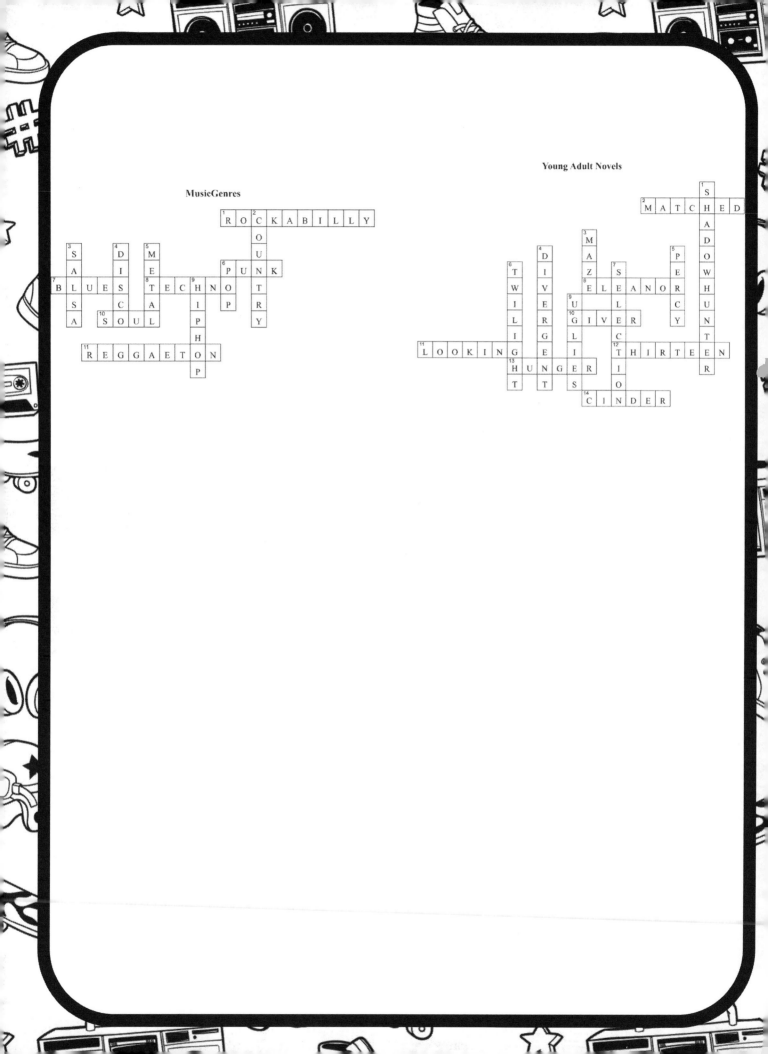

Thank you for your purchase

I hope you enjoy the book as much
as we did making it,
please consider leaving a
review on Amazon

As a small independent author
reviews really help other
people make informed
purchases.

Please Enjoy

Made in the USA
Columbia, SC
10 December 2024

48934505R00059